Environment and Development

TITLES OF RELATED INTEREST

Environment and Development

PETER BARTELMUS

Boston
ALLEN & UNWIN
London   Sydney

The author is a staff member of the United Nations. The views expressed
in this book are his own and not necessarily those of the United Nations.

Allen & Unwin Inc.,
8 Winchester Place, Winchester, Mass. 01890, USA

Allen & Unwin (Publishers) Ltd,
40 Museum Street, London WC1A 1LU, UK

Allen & Unwin (Publishers) Ltd,
Park Lane, Hemel Hempstead, Herts HP2 4TE, UK

Allen & Unwin (Australia) Ltd,
8 Napier Street, North Sydney, NSW 2060, Australia

First published in 1986

Library of Congress Cataloging in Publication Data

Bartelmus, Peter.
    Environment and development.
Bibliography: p.
Includes index.
1. Environmental policy – Developing countries.
2. Developing countries – Economic policy.   I. Title.
HC59.72.E5B37   1986   333.7′09172′4   85-22838
ISBN 0-04-333026-6 (alk. paper)
ISBN 0-04-333022-3 (pbk.: alk. paper)

British Library Cataloguing in Publication Data

Bartelmus, Peter
    Environment and development.
1. City planning – Developing countries
2. Regional planning – Developing countries.
I. Title
711′.3′091724   HT169.5
ISBN 0-04-333026-6
ISBN 0-04-333022-6 Pbk

Set in 11 on 13 point Bembo by Computape (Pickering) Ltd, North
Yorkshire and printed in Great Britain by Anchor Brendon Ltd,
Tiptree, Essex

ສົ້
ຣິລາ

Preface

The Earth's finite natural resources have been exploited for centuries. Only over the past two decades, however, has public attention been caught by serious phenomena of resource depletion and scarcity. Widespread concern about environmental degradation has also been expressed in conjunction with conspicuous pollution incidents in the 1960s. Zero growth of the economy and the population was then postulated in industrialized countries to avoid the disastrous transgression of the physical "outer limits" of the planet. Developing countries remained only peripherally interested, considering environmental concerns to be marginal products of high-level economic growth. Today, environmental problems are generally seen to stem both from economic growth and from activities induced by an actual lack of development. The term "pollution of poverty" has been widely used in reference to the recent concern with the environment in developing countries.

International organizations have encouraged the opening of a dialogue on the environment between economically developed and developing countries. However, various industrialized countries seem to have dissociated themselves from their initial position of environmental heralds in a reassessment of priorities relative to economic and environmental issues. Developing nations on the other hand continue to be concerned with the environment, particularly with respect to their resource base and life-support systems.

Despite the continuing efforts of international organizations to promote environmental issues, no generally recognized model of the relationships between environment and development is available. Some international agreement on development objectives and policy measures, which include environmental aspects, has been reached through the adoption of the International Development Strategy for the Third United Nations Development Decade. However, the outlook for the implementation of this strategy is bleak. The failure, so far, to initiate a round of global negotiations for the implementation of a New International Economic Order does not augur well for the success of the Third Development Decade.

At the national level, development policies frequently follow a muddle-through approach, as environmental, social and sometimes even economic objectives and priorities are neglected or affected by political pressures rather than substantive knowledge. To some extent this can be explained by the resistance of dominant classes in countries to implementing strategies that might impair their privileges. But there is also confusion about the appropriate style of development because of discrepancies between values and cultures in developing countries and international development concepts and strategies that are largely based on the life-styles and technologies of northern industrialized countries. The need for alternative development has been reiterated, but opinions differ widely as to its contents and implementation.

This book focuses therefore on exploring the environment–development problematique at the national and subnational levels. It reviews what is known about environmental problems in developing countries and what can be done by the countries themselves to tackle them. The text is organized into four major themes: concepts and definitions, assessment of environmental problems, planning for solving these problems, and plan implementation.

In Chapter 1, the basic concepts of environment and development are discussed. There follows a description of the intrinsic relationships between environment and development. Some of the more extreme views of the environment are highlighted, and the efforts of international organizations to develop a balanced view of environment and development are outlined. The main environmental concerns of developing countries are presented in Chapter 2. It is shown that while the industrialized, agrarian, market and non-market economies all face similar environmental problems, the scale and intensity of these problems, as well as the priorities assigned to environmental, social and economic concerns, vary considerably among countries.

Starting from a basic framework of human interactions with ecosystems, the concept of ecodevelopment is introduced in the third chapter. Ecodevelopment is set forth as a basic approach to the integration of environment with development planning. Various models of ecodevelopment, ecostrategies and ecotechniques are presented. The application of different planning concepts and strategies to the solution of environmental problems is discussed in Chapter 4. Following a review of the reasons for typical plan failures, possibilities of injecting environmental criteria into the centralized planning system are highlighted. As an alternative to central planning, ecodevelopment is advocated, and the ways and means of implementing this approach at local levels are outlined.

Peter Bartelmus

Acknowledgements

I would like to thank the following individuals and organizations who have given permission for the reproduction of copyright material:

Weltforum Verlag (Fig. 1.2); United Nations Educational, Scientific and Cultural Organization (Fig. 2.1); United Nations and Pergamon Press Ltd. (Fig. 2.4); International Institute for Applied Systems Analysis (Fig. 3.3); Food and Agriculture Organization of the United Nations (Fig. 3.4); Statistisk Sentralbyrå (Fig. 4.1); Table 3.1 reproduced from *Ecologic–economic analysis for regional development* by W. Isard *et al.* (1972) by permission of The Free Press, a Division of Macmillan Inc.; Academic Press (Table 3.2); International Union for Conservation of Nature and Natural Resources (Table 3.3); Organization of American States (Table 4.1). Acknowledgements to photographers and photo agencies are given in the plate captions.

Contents

List of tables

List of plates

Abbreviations

CBA	cost-benefit analysis
ENDA	Environmental Development Action in the Third World
EIA	environmental impact assessment
FAO	Food and Agriculture Organization of the United Nations
GDP	gross domestic product
GEMS	Global Environment Monitoring System
GNP	gross national product
ILO	International Labor Organization
IRPTC	International Register of Potentially Toxic Chemicals
IUCN	International Union for Conservation of Nature and Natural Resources
LDC	least-developed countries
MAB	Programme on Man and the Biosphere
NIC	newly industrialized countries
OAS	Organization of American States
OECD	Organisation for Economic Co-operation and Development
SCOPE	Scientific Committee on Problems of the Environment (of the International Council of Scientific Unions)
UNCTAD	United Nations Conference on Trade and Development
UN/ECE	United Nations/Economic Commission for Europe
UN/ESCAP	United Nations/Economic and Social Commission for Asia and the Pacific
UNEP	United Nations Environment Programme

UNESCO	United Nations Educational, Scientific and Cultural Organization
UNIDO	United Nations Industrial Development Organization
WHO	World Health Organization
WMO	World Meteorological Organization

1 Concepts: environment and development

Scope and components of the human environment

Ecologists have generally defined the environment as the external conditions and influences affecting the life and development of organisms. From this basic concept a definition of the *human environment* can be derived by replacing "organisms" by "man" in the above definition. Further clarification of the nature of human conditions and influences is needed.

Taking a global look at the whole of mankind, regional variations of habitat may be put aside for a description of the major physical characteristics of our planet. The *lithosphere* includes the Earth's solid crust down to an average depth of 60 km into the interior of the globe. The *hydrosphere* is made up by the oceans, lakes, rivers, icecaps and other water bodies. The *atmosphere* comprises the gaseous envelope of the planet (Fig. 1.1). The *biosphere* is the part of the physical world where life can exist, and includes the living organisms themselves. It extends into all other "spheres" and is usually broken down into biotic and abiotic components. Living organisms and non-living parts depend upon each other and interact in complex ways which are studied by ecologists with the fundamental ecosystem approach. Continuous energy flows to and from the planet are truly vital for all processes within the biosphere; they open and link our environment, beyond the physical world of the atmosphere, hydrosphere and lithosphere, to the far-off Sun.

Moving from the global view of "spaceship Earth" (Boulding 1966) to a regional, national or local level, one is led to the consideration of fellow human beings as an

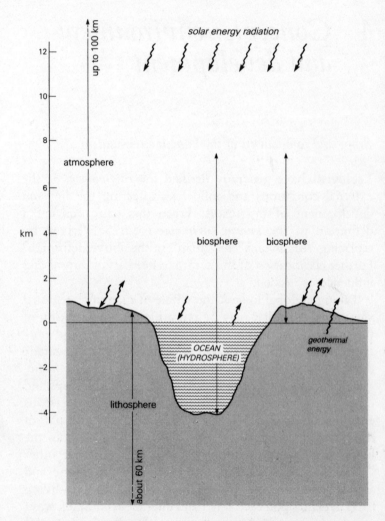

Figure 1.1 The physical world.

additional social component of the environment. Social groups such as nations, tribes and families interact in numerous ways, both aggressive and cooperative, and cause distinctive impacts, both productive and destructive, on the biophysical environment. In particular, they have created an artificial, man-made environment which affects all other environmental components. The environmental problem exists within these inter-relationships and inter-dependencies.

What is development?

Development is generally accepted to be a process that attempts to improve the living conditions of people. Most also agree that the improvement of living conditions relates to non-material wants as well as to physical requirements. Development goals that call for the increase of human welfare or the improvement of the quality of life reflect this agreement.

Quantifiable definitions of these concepts are needed for measuring progress toward development goals. A typical starting point has been to break down the overall objective of human welfare into sub-objectives or targets. The difficulties involved are described by Bartelmus (1980, p. 40 *et seq.*), who offers a tentative list of general human objectives, condensed from a variety of publicly pro-claimed social objectives. The list of objectives includes affection, recreation and entertainment, education, human freedoms (security), shelter, esthetic and cultural values, political equity (participation and social opportunities), health, physiological needs and future quality of life. Sub-jective value judgements are involved in such a list, and any further breakdown would be even more arbitrary as human preferences vary significantly among individuals and through time and space.

Generally applicable policies and strategies to meet such objectives are as difficult to identify as the objectives themselves. Such policies must weigh conflicting goals and values, within varying socioeconomic conditions. In most developing nations, low levels of living and produc-tivity are accompanied by high levels of population growth, unemployment, international dependence and a predominantly agrarian base to the economy. Based on these common factors, some international agreement on development strategies has been reached but has had to be revised in view of considerable failures of such strategies at the national level.

The United Nations First Development Decade of the 1960s was based on the belief that the fruits of accelerated economic growth would trickle down to the low-income population strata. Since the trickle-down effect did not succeed in alleviating poverty in developing countries, the objective of social justice was added to the objectives formulated for the Second Development Decade. An improved distribution of the results of economic growth was aimed at. The International Development Strategy for the Third United Nations Development Decade of the 1980s proceeds from the recognition that the objectives of the Second Decade were not met because of inequities and imbalances in international economic relations. The new strategy, therefore, includes the aim of establishing a New International Economic Order (adopted by the General Assembly of the United Nations in 1974) in its basic goal of accelerated development. This concern with an international order might help to correct international imbalances; however, it might also draw attention away from national inequities that, after all, were to be alleviated by the strategy of the Second Development Decade.

At the national level, three basic paradigms of development can be identified (Jolly 1977). The *neoclassical growth model* focuses on individual planning, market mechanisms, and increased saving and capital injection by foreign aid for investment. The model was soon abandoned, however, because of structural and institutional constraints to economic growth in developing countries, such as the absence of markets and infrastructure, the influence of internal and external power structures, and a prevailing lack of know-how. Consequently, models for structural change and reform emerged, reflecting the ideologies of centrally planned (socialist) or market (capitalist) economies.

The *neo-Marxist structuralist model* advocates central planning based on state ownership and control. Structural and institutional change is to be achieved by breaking away from feudalism and capitalism for the establishment of a socialist society. By contrast, the *capitalistic structuralist model* favors indicative planning accompanied by structural and institutional reform such as land reform and a certain measure of control over industry and multinationals. The major development goal is the redistribution of the fruits of accelerated economic growth. Based on the structural paradigms, the *dependency theories* of development view the world as consisting of a "core" of dominant nations and a "periphery" of dependent ones. Dependency theories thus stress external (political, economic and technological) influences as the major reasons for widespread underdevelopment (Seers 1981, p. 15).

All the above paradigms advocate a center-down approach to the implementation of development strategies. The failure of this approach to reach the poor at the bottom of society has led to the search for alternative "bottom-up" strategies, especially for the least-developed countries. Such development from below focuses on the satisfaction of the basic needs of the poorest people at the local level through the mobilization of all natural, human and institutional resources in small territorial units (Stöhr 1981).

Which are the developing countries?

An appropriate yardstick of development has yet to be contrived to identify nations as "developing." Such a yardstick would also facilitate the ranking or grouping of countries according to the stage of development that has been reached. The economic-growth concept of development utilizes gross domestic or national product as a concise measure of development, usually calculated in per-capita and real (price-deflated) terms. For a multidisciplinary concept of development, as expressed in lists of human objectives or needs, it is more difficult to find a

Table 1.1 Developing countries[a] by GDP per capita (US $ 1979[b]), country profiles (C, D, E) and UN-LDC criteria (asterisk).

$100-199	$200-299	$300-399	$400-499	$500-999	$1000-1499
* Bangladesh (E)	* Afghanistan [1978] (E)	* Central African Republic (E)	Angola (E)	* Benin (E)	Algeria[e] (D)
* Bhutan (E)	* Chad (E)	* Democratic Yemen (E)	Dominica	Bolivia (D)	* Botswana (D)
* Burkina Faso (E)	* Comoros	Guinea (E)	Egypt (C)	Congo [1978] (D)	Chile (C)
* Burma [1978] (D)	* Gambia (E)	Indonesia (D)	Grenada (C)	El Salvador (D)	Colombia (D)
* Burundi (E)	* Guinea-Bissau (E)	Kenya (D)	Lebanon (C)	Ghana (D)	* Djibouti
Democratic Kampuchea	* Haiti (E)	Madagascar (D)	Liberia (E)	Guatemala (C)	Dominican Republic (C)
* Equatorial Guinea (E)	India (E)	Mauritania (D)	* Samoa	Guyana (C)	Ecuador (D)
* Ethiopia (E)	* Malawi (E)	* Niger (E)	Senegal (E)	Honduras (D)	Ivory Coast (D)
* Lao People's Democratic Republic[c] (E)	Mozambique (E)	Sierra Leone (D)	Solomon Islands	Jordan (C)	Jamaica (C)
* Lesotho[d] (E)	Pakistan (D)		Togo (E)	Morocco (D)	Mauritius (C)
* Mali (E)	* Rwanda (E)		* Uganda [1978] (E)	Nicaragua (C)	Paraguay (C)
* Nepal (E)	* Somalia (E)		* Yemen (E)	Nigeria (D)	Syrian Arab Republic (C)
* Upper Volta (E)	Sri Lanka (C)			Papua New Guinea (D)	Tunisia (D)
	* United Republic of Tanzania (E)			Peru (C)	Turkey [1978] (C)
	Zaire (E)			Philippines (D)	
				Saint Lucia	
				Saint Vincent and the Grenadines	
				* Sudan (E)	
				Swaziland (D)	
				Thailand (C)	
				United Republic of Cameroon (D)	
				Vanuatu	
				Zambia (D)	
				Zimbabwe (C)	

Sources: GDP per capita: United Nations (1981); country profiles: McHale and McHale (1977); LDC: UNCTAD (1984). [a] Excluding Eastern European Socialist Countries and Bahamas (C), *Cape Verde, China (C), Cuba (C), Mongolia (C), *Sao Tome and Principe, Viet Nam (C) and the NIC Brazil (C), Hong Kong (B), Mexico (B), Singapore (B), South Korea (C), Taiwan (C). [b] Other years in brackets. [c] GDP per capita: $99. [d] GDP per capita: $81. [e] GDP per capita: $1639.

similar aggregate measure. The development of social indicators and the correction of national accounting aggregates to obtain measures of economic welfare are still in their infancy; they cannot replace national product, which provides an overall insight into a country's productive capabilities, and hence into its major source of national welfare.

Three approaches to classifying countries according to their stage of development are compared in Table 1.1. The basic grouping is determined by the traditional measure of gross domestic product (GDP) per capita. A multi-indicator classification, averaging about 125 variables into five categories (from *A* for the richest to *E* for the least-developed countries), is indicated in brackets for most countries. In addition, the United Nations specification of least-developed countries (LDC) is indicated by an asterisk; it is based on per-capita GDP combined with indicators of manufacturing and literacy, and is finally determined by resolutions of the United Nations General Assembly. The table shows a distinct correlation of all classifications for the lowest ($100–299) group. The three classifications differ considerably, however, in the $300–499 group. At least for this income bracket, the traditional economic measures seem to overemphasize the productive aspects of welfare at the expense of social, cultural and environmental concerns. The ranking of Table 1.1 excludes the newly industrializing countries, or NIC (Brazil, South Korea, Hong Kong, Singapore, Mexico and Taiwan), which enjoyed sustained and rapid economic growth backed up by industrialization and exportation of industrial commodities.

Environment and economic process

A close connection between environment and development is implicit in the definitions of the environment (as the conditions and influences that interact with man) and of development (as a process to improve human welfare) just arrived at. The environment can be considered to be an

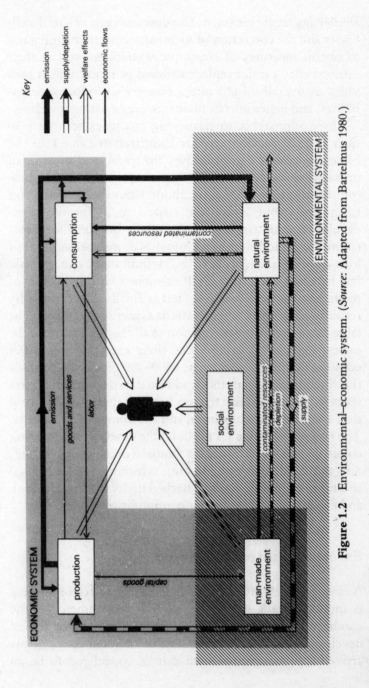

Key

→ emission

→ supply/depletion

⇒ welfare effects

⇒ economic flows

ECONOMIC SYSTEM

consumption

contaminated resources

goods and services

labor

social environment

emission

production

capital goods

ENVIRONMENTAL SYSTEM

natural environment

contaminated resources

natural resources

depletion

supply

man-made environment

Figure 1.2 Environmental–economic system. (*Source:* Adapted from Bartelmus 1980.)

integral part of development, since any impact on man's environment also influences his state of wellbeing or welfare. Environment and development are thus linked together so intricately that separate approaches to either environmental or developmental problems are piecemeal at best. In the past, just such an approach has typically been followed, and tools of decision-making have been developed and used independently in the fields of economic development and environment. An analysis of the interrelationships between the environmental and economic systems will confirm the need for integrated policies.

The economic system comprises productive, consumptive and accumulative activities which create flows of goods and services (including labor) between the system components. The environmental system consists of natural, man-made and social components. In Figure 1.2, the two systems are shown to overlap in the area of the man-made environment, which is depicted as the result of capital formation. Emissions of wastes or pollutants originating from production and consumption activities are indicated by bold black arrows. Flows of natural resources to production and consumption are shown as broken arrows. These flows represent the two basic functions of the natural environment: waste disposal from and resource supply to the economic system. This presentation is based on the principle of mass conservation, according to which resources may be used but are never consumed. All materials either return to the natural environment or are recycled into the economic process, generally in a modified form. Recycling is, therefore, the only ecologically sound way of waste disposal. Recycling is indicated explicitly in the flow chart by feedback loops of emissions. Destructive ("disastrous") activities of the natural environment are symbolized as depletion flows from the man-made to the natural environment, and out of the natural environment.

Environmental and economic activities may affect human welfare either positively or negatively. This is indicated in the figure by white arrows pointing from all economic and environmental components to the symbol for man. The consumption of "useful" goods and services provides individuals with what economists call "utility" or "wellbeing." Toxic goods (or rather toxic "bads"), such as contaminating pollutants, impair human health. Active participation in the productive system may produce either positive or negative effects resulting from job satisfaction or stress. Marginal settlements are a source of much misery, while adequate shelter and other man-made facilities can contribute to a sense of security, wellbeing and self-esteem. The impacts of aggressive and altruistic actions of individuals and social groups are indicated as welfare effects of the social environment. And, though nature is a source of joy and recreation, it can also be a hazard in the case of natural disasters.

Economic theory has attempted to deal with these effects as externalities. *Externalities* are usually defined as unintentional side effects of production and consumption that affect the levels of consumer utility and enterprise costs. The logical approach to dealing with these external effects is to internalize them into the price–cost structure of the economy by means of taxes, subsidies or other market incentives. The resulting, revised price system is expected to ensure the reallocation of resources in an optimal way. The "polluter-pays principle" widely advocated in industrialized market economies is based on this approach (OECD 1975). Such a marginal (price–cost corrective) approach has not been able to provide a general solution to the environmental problem. First, the complexity and magnitude of environmental problems give rise to enormous social costs which are beyond the internalization capabilities of individual households or enterprises. Second, market imperfections resulting from national and international power structures and transboundary environmental impacts prevent an optimal allocation of resources, making the internalization of environmental costs and benefits quite meaningless for purposes of resource distribution.

Environment and development: the international discussion

The failure of traditional economic theory and policy to prevent or remedy environmental degradation led to the appearance of the "doomsday view" of the environmental problem. Zero (or even negative) growth was advocated to avoid the disastrous consequences of transgressing the physical limits of the Earth's resources. Another pessimistic "conservationist" view focused on the preservation of ecosystems and endangered species to the neglect of socioeconomic conditions and consequences. These policies could not be accepted by countries that were still in the early stages of socioeconomic development. These countries considered growth to be more important than the concern about endangered species of wildlife. It was thought that only more affluent countries could afford the luxury of diverting some of their wealth to environmental protection. Moreover, the high and wasteful consumption levels of the industrialized nations placed a large stress on the resources of developing countries. Proclamations of global solidarity for spaceship Earth were thus met with suspicion and distrust by the developing nations. The only view rich and poor countries seemed to share was the conviction that environmental conservation and economic development are in conflict with each other (UNEP 1978). It is the merit of the international community that it has opened a dialogue on the environment-and-development issue between developed and developing countries through a number of international seminars and conferences.

The Secretariat for the United Nations Conference on the Human Environment organized a seminar on development and environment at Founex, Switzerland (United Nations Conference on the Human Environment 1972). The seminar concluded that environmental problems do not only result from the development process itself but also from the very lack of development. Poor water, inadequate housing and sanitation, malnutrition, disease and natural disasters were cited as important examples. The term "pollution of poverty" was later used to describe this aspect of the environmental question. Consequently, it was suggested that environmental goals provide a new dimension to the development concept itself, requiring an integrated approach to environment and development.

The United Nations Conference on the Human Environment (United Nations 1973) endorsed these principles, emphasizing that most environmental problems in developing countries are caused by underdevelopment and that environmental and developmental goals could be harmonized, *inter alia*, by the wise use of natural resources. The concept of underdevelopment was not further elaborated but the mention of it can be taken as a reference to the historic exploitation of human and natural resources by the colonial powers. The Declaration of the Stockholm Conference thus includes the elimination of colonial and other forms of oppression as the number-one principle. Eight years later, however, an investigation of the worldwide North–South relations found that the process of decolonization was not complete, and countries were still fighting for political as well as economic and cultural independence (Brandt 1980).

In the wake of the energy crises in 1973 and 1974 and of the declaration of the New International Economic Order in 1974, a joint UNEP/UNCTAD Symposium at Cocoyoc attempted to integrate a general assessment of development goals with new ideas in the field of environment. It was recognized that the failure of society to provide a safe and happy life for all is not one of "absolute physical shortage but of economic and social maldistribution and misuse." Development, in the sense of growth of economic macro-indicators, had not succeeded in alleviating the situation of the poorest people. Hence, the symposium advocated a strategy of satisfying first the basic needs of man, with due consideration for global environmental risks or so-called "outer limits." For those resources that do not fall under national jurisdiction, the global commons, the establishment of a strong international regime was recommended (UNEP & UNCTAD 1974). The basic-needs approach was again taken up and widely publicized by the Programme of Action of the 1976 World Employment Conference. The Programme recognized food, shelter, clothing and essential services such as safe drinking water, sanitation, transport, health and education as basic human needs and requested that basic-needs policies become an essential part of the United Nations Third Development Decade Strategy (ILO 1977).

More recently, international statements have tended to dissociate themselves from the basic-needs approach. As shown in various national contributions to international meetings, the strong support of this strategy by developed nations has been considered to be a tactical move to divert attention away from the implementation of the New International Economic Order. In addition, it was felt that an international strategy concentrating only on the satisfaction of basic needs represents an intrusion into sovereign national development policies which may have other priorities, such as building an infrastructure for industrialization.

Thus the International Development Strategy for the Third Development Decade omits any reference to the satisfaction of basic human needs, stressing instead the establishment of a New International Economic Order as an integral part of international efforts to accelerate the development of poor countries. The strategy also mentions explicitly the inter-relationships between environment, development, population and natural resources as well as environmental degradation in urban slums. In addition, it requests the prevention of deforestation, erosion, soil degradation and desertification. Corresponding policy measures should promote the ecological soundness of developmental activities *inter alia* by intensified research into the environment and development relationship.

The most important outcome of the international discussion is the recognition that the overall goals of environment and development are not in conflict but are indeed the same, namely the improvement of the human quality of life or welfare for present and future generations. Phrases like the "integrated approach to environment and development," "sustainable and environmentally sound development," and "alternative patterns of development and lifestyles" reflect the need for integration of environmental dimensions into development planning and strategies. To what extent and in which way these views can be implemented by developing nations depends on the national perception of the environmental problem, the political will to pursue environmental strategies, the tools available to implement strategies, and the specific environmental conditions and problems of countries. The next chapter will focus on this last point, namely an assessment of the major environmental problems in the less-developed regions of the world, before embarking on the constraints and opportunities of environmentally sound development planning and policies.

Suggestions for further reading

Concepts of development   Despite the various international attempts to achieve agreement about development strategies, uncertainty about the meaning of "development" prevails in the light of significant failures of these strategies at the national level. Some conflicting viewpoints are highlighted in the responses to an OECD survey (Birou *et al.* 1977). Doubts about the applicability of the conventional development paradigms are expressed by Jolly (1977). Similar skepticism about the "planning mystique" of development policy has been expressed by Todaro (1977). A critical review of the dependency theory of development is given in Seers (1981).

Another development, stressing human needs and ecological soundness in satisfying them, is advocated by the Dag Hammarskjöld project (Nerfin 1977). Riddell (1981) distinguishes between overdevelopment (characterized by wasteful consumption) in industrialized northern countries and underdevelopment of southern countries (resulting from past and current imperialism of northern countries). He suggests bypassing both the neo-Marxist and capitalistic models of economic growth and industrialization to achieve social progress through "ecodevelopment." Seers (1983) stresses the failure of the development paradigms to take into account the rising nationalism of developing countries which react against neocolonial manipulation; he suggests that this nationalism be extended into the formation of regional power blocs to replace the neocolonial system. The feasibility of "development from below" as an alternative to the dominant "from above" approach to regional development planning is examined in Stöhr and Taylor (1981).

Basic-needs approach to development In addition to the theoretical studies cited in the text, a quantitative global assessment of basic human needs has been undertaken by the McHales (1977). A more systematic approach linking basic needs and environmental limits in an activity-analysis model is suggested by Bartelmus (1979a). Some general policy issues surrounding the basic-needs model are dealt with by Soedjatmoko (1979). Stokes (1978) asserts that the basic human needs can only be met through the participation of individuals and communities at local levels.

The dissociation of the international community from the basic-needs approach as the fundamental principle of development strategies can be seen in various contributions to international meetings, especially those of the United Nations General Assembly and the Committee for Development Planning of the United Nations Economic and Social Council. Invariably, these contributions are made in reference to the New International Economic Order (Resolution 3201 and 3202 of the Sixth Special Session of the General Assembly of the United Nations) and the International Development Strategy (Resolution 35/56 of the Thirty-fifth Session of the General Assembly of the United Nations).

Social indicators and welfare measurement   The development of social indicators of the quality of human life, as compared to the quantitative measures of economic growth, is described by Bartelmus (1980). The author also attempts to assess the environmental component of economic welfare. Suggestions for defining and measuring economic welfare by means of correcting national accounts aggregates have been advanced by Sametz (1968) and Nordhaus and Tobin (1973). Important descriptions of social indicators are the list of social concerns of the OECD (1973) and a comparative listing of indicators by the United Nations (1978a).

Doomsday views and conservationist approaches   The following selected titles are good indicators of the authors' views of the environmental problem:

> *The death of tomorrow* (Loraine 1972)
> *Ecological crisis: readings for survival* (Love & Love 1970)
> *Ein Planet wird geplündert. Die Schreckensbilanz unserer Politik* (Gruhl 1975)
> *Silent spring* (Carson 1965)
> *Blueprint for survival* (Goldsmith *et al.* 1972).

The use of a seemingly objective computerized global model was probably responsible for provoking much of the widespread attention to the Club of Rome's "Limits to growth" (Meadows *et al.* 1972). The model predicts a "rather sudden and uncontrollable decline in both population and industrial capacity" within the next century, if current growth trends remain unchanged. A critical review of the model and its basic assumptions is offered by Cole *et al.* (1973).

Examples of the "conservationist" view of the natural environment include: Curry-Lindahl (1972), who devotes half a page out of over 300 to "environment and development;" Dasmann (1963), who admits subjectiveness and one-sidedness on some issues; and Caldwell (1972), who purports to defend Earth against the "unecological animal" man.

Environment as an externality A definition of externalities and a description of their relationship to general economic equilibrium and Pareto optimality can be found in most textbooks of micro-economic theory. Ayres (1978) reviews the treatment of the environment in models of economic theory including general equilibrium and material–energy flows models. Externalities in the context of cost–benefit analyses, which frequently deal with environmental impacts, are described by Das Gupta and Pearce (1972) and Cooper (1981). An outline of the relationships between environmental non-market effects, externalities and public goods is given by Bartelmus (1980) and, from a more economic point of view, by Pearce (1976). The "polluter-pays principle" has been advocated, in particular, by the OECD, for environmental policy in its member countries (OECD 1975).

2 Assessment: environmental trends in developing countries

Rich and poor: similar concerns – differing priorities

Chapter 1 described environmental degradation as impacts from human interaction with the natural, social and man-made environment. This general explanation applies to both economically developed and less developed societies. The international discussion revealed that many environmental problems in developing countries originate from the lack of development, that is from the struggle to overcome extreme conditions of poverty. In industrialized countries, on the other hand, impacts of economic growth are responsible in most cases for environmental deterioration. There is also a difference in the significance of environmental impacts: wealthy countries face a deterioration of the quality of life, but life itself may be at stake in developing nations when their natural resource base is destroyed.

A number of international surveys, seminars and studies have been undertaken for the world-wide assessment of the state and trends of the environment. Invariably, the large data gaps, especially in developing countries, are deplored in these surveys. International monitoring and data-collection programs have been established to rectify this situation (see the "further reading" suggestions). The results of these surveys and studies suggest that most environmental impacts can be observed in the developing as well as the developed regions of the world. Environmental problems vary, however, in scope and intensity. Consequently, they receive differing priorities in national planning and policy-making.

Table 2.1 Environmental concerns of developing and industrialized countries.

Environmental concerns	Developing countries	Industrialized countries
I Natural environment		
A Air	Air pollution in major cities	AIR POLLUTION
B Land, soil, mineral resources (incl. energy)	SOIL EROSION AND DEGRADATION, DESERTIFICATION	Soil loss and deterioration; dumping of waste; risk of radioactive contamination from nuclear-power production
C Water	FRESHWATER SHORTAGE; freshwater pollution (sewage, pesticides); pollution of coastal waters	Freshwater shortage; INLAND AND MARINE WATER POLLUTION
D Fauna and flora	DEFORESTATION (especially of tropical forests); loss of genetic resources; endangered species	Loss of genetic resources; endangered species
E Ecosystems	Pollution of coastal ecosystems (decreasing fish catch)	Disruption of mountain, wetland, freshwater (especially from acid rains and eutrophication) and coastal ecosystems
F Natural disasters	FLOODS; DROUGHTS; STORMS; earthquakes, volcanic eruptions	Floods; earthquakes
II Man-made environment and living conditions		
A Bioproductive systems	LOSS AND DEGRADATION OF ARABLE LAND; pests and pest resistance; water shortage; pressures on fish population (overfishing, pollution); IMPACTS OF FUELWOOD CONSUMPTION, food contamination, post-harvest losses	Loss of croplands to urban sprawl; pests and pest resistance; contamination of crops and fish; over-exploitation of fishing grounds
B Human settlements	MARGINAL SETTLEMENTS (RURAL–URBAN MIGRATION, URBAN GROWTH)	URBAN SPRAWL; NOISE
C Health	MAL- AND UNDERNUTRITION; INFECTIOUS AND PARASITIC DISEASES	CANCER; cardiovascular diseases; genetic and long-term effects of POTENTIALLY TOXIC CHEMICALS

Source: See suggestions for further reading, Chapter 2.

Table 2.1 summarizes the issues discussed in major international surveys and assessments of the state of the environment, pointing out (by capital letters) those concerns that have been stressed to be of particular significance. The depletion and degradation of natural resources (land/soil, water and forests) and their effects on food and energy supply, marginal conditions in human settlements, and environmentally conditioned diseases are high-priority issues in developing countries. By contrast, industrialized countries are especially concerned with air and water pollution and the long-term health effects of toxic chemicals.

Major environmental problems in developing countries

The predominantly agricultural economies of developing countries depend on the availability and quality of natural resources for the sustained use of the bioproductive systems of agriculture, ranching, forestry and fishery. Degradation and depletion of land/soil, water and forests are thus the outstanding environmental problems of developing countries. The inability of bioproductive systems to produce sufficient food for rapidly growing populations is the cause of perhaps the greatest scourge of mankind – hunger and malnutrition. The United Nations World Food Council (1977, p. 3) estimated that about 500 million people, 95 percent of whom are in developing countries, live at a nutritional level below minimum acceptable standards. Over 2 million deaths were caused by famine in the 1970s, according to an estimate by the Worldwatch Institute (Brown *et al.* 1984, p. 188). Little improvement of this situation can be expected for the least-developed countries, since food output will be hardly above population growth: per-capita consumption is predicted to decline in sub-Saharan developing countries, to stagnate in South Asia, Northern Africa and the Middle East, and to increase only in Latin America and East Asia (Council on Environmental Quality 1980, p. 17).

Table 2.2 Soil degradation in major regions.

Region	Arable land 1975 (million ha)	Annual sediment discharge per ha of arable land (billion t per year)	Percentage of salinized and alkalinized areas[a] over arable land (%)	Percentage of area affected by desertification over area of irrigated land, rainfed cropland and range land (%)
Asia	349.6[b]	41.6	31.2[b]	81.4[c]
Latin America	176.8	6.2	74.0	82.3
Africa	205.0	2.3	39.3	86.3

Source: FAO; Robinson; Szaboles; United Nations, as cited in Holdgate *et al.* (1982, pp. 254, 266, 268–9, 272).
[a] Most affected countries only.
[b] Excluding China.
[c] Including USSR.

Table 2.3 Annual erosion of topsoil in excess of new soil formation.

	Total cropland (million ha)	Excessive soil loss (million ha)	Excessive soil loss per ha of cropland (t per ha)
USA	16 520	1 500	9.1
USSR	24 800	2 300	9.3
India	13 840	4 700	34.0
China	9 800	3 300	33.7
rest of the world	59 920	10 900	18.2
total	124 920	22 700	18.2

Source: Worldwatch Institute estimates (presented in Brown *et al.* 1984, p. 62).

Increasing world food demand exerts mounting pressures on *land* which is the major factor of production in agriculture. Land is degraded and loses its productive capacity through soil erosion, salinization, alkalinization, waterlogging and chemical degradation. If land is degraded permanently in semi-arid and arid areas, desertification takes place (Plate 2.1). Other significant losses of agricultural land are brought about by changing land use, especially by the expansion of human settlements and large-scale infrastructure. If current losses of agricultural land continue, the total area of high-productivity cropland will decrease by 55 million hectares by the year 2000, through toxification and conversion to non-agricultural use (Buringh as cited by Holdgate *et al.* 1982, p. 255).

Table 2.2 indicates the extent of overall soil degradation in major regions in which developing countries are situated. It does not show, however, the large variation within these regions. Soil erosion (in terms of annual discharge of sediments) is by far the highest in Asia. Table 2.3 gives an estimate of actual soil loss from croplands for the four major food-producing countries. Salinization and alkalinization of soils seem to be the major problems in Latin America. Desertification occurs to a similar extent in all regions. It is estimated that some 60 000 km^2 of land are

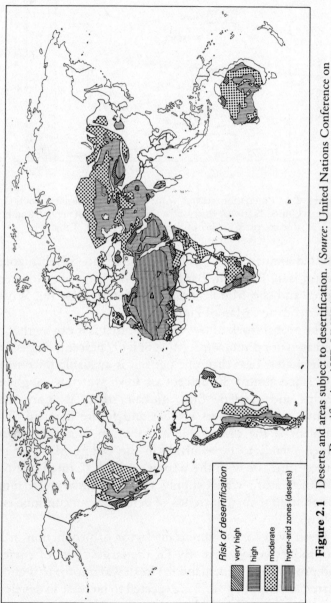

Figure 2.1 Deserts and areas subject to desertification. (*Source*: United Nations Conference on Desertification 1977: UNEP/FAO/UNESCO/WMO.)

Risk of desertification

very high

high

moderate

hyper-arid zones (deserts)

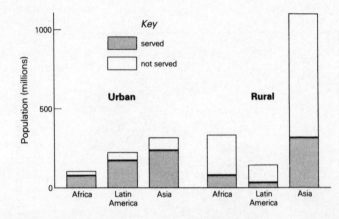

Figure 2.2 Population served with water in developing countries. (*Source*: United Nations, thirty-fifth session of the General Assembly, document A/35/367 of September 18, 1980, Table 3.)

affected annually, especially in the Sudano–Sahelian zone, Brazil, Iran, Pakistan, Bangladesh, Afghanistan, Northern Africa and the Middle East, as illustrated by the World Desertification Map of Figure 2.1.

The global stock of *water* is fixed, that is it can neither be increased nor diminished. Most of it (97 percent) consists of ocean water. Less than one percent is available for human use, since almost 80 percent of fresh water is caught in icecaps and glaciers. Still, globally there is more than enough water to meet present and future demand. The problem is the inequitable distribution of the resource, which "tends to be available in the wrong place, at the wrong time, or with the wrong quality" (United Nations 1978b). Future water supply might become even more destabilized if current trends of deforestation continue (see below).

Fresh water is an important factor of production in all bioproductive systems. By far the largest part of current and projected total demand for fresh water is for irrigation. Water scarcity (Plate 2.2) is expected to increase in developing countries, affecting both consumption by humans and irrigation (Council on Environmental Quality 1980, p. 26).

Table 2.4 Area of annual deforestation of closed broad-leaved forest in tropical regions.

| | 1976–80 | | 1981–85 | |
	('000 ha)	(%)	('000 ha)	(%)
tropical Americas	3807	55	4006	56
tropical Africa	1319	19	1318	19
tropical Asia	1767	26	1782	25
total	6893	100	7106	100

Source: Lanly (1982, p. 82).

Irrigation frequently reduces soil productivity through salinization and waterlogging and causes the spread of water-related diseases such as malaria and schistosomiasis. Figure 2.2 shows the relatively low supply of drinking water to the rural areas in developing countries. Of course, the situation varies considerably not only from region to region but also among countries within regions.

Forests are a vital bioproductive system. They provide lumber, fuel and habitat for a multitude of species; they also protect soils and regulate water balances and climates. The world's forests have been reduced by probably more than one-third (Holdgate *et al.* 1982, p. 213) in the search for additional agricultural land and wood for shelter and energy. Particularly affected by deforestation are the tropical forests of less-developed countries (Plate 2.3). Table 2.4 shows that more than half of tropical-forest depletion takes place in the tropical Americas. For 1981–85, an increase in the rate of depletion of about five percent has been forecast for this area, while depletion will continue at about the same level in the other areas. It is estimated that by the year 2020 virtually all the accessible forests in developing countries will have been cut (Council on Environment Quality 1980, p. 26). Environmental impacts of deforestation are particularly conspicuous on the slopes of the Himalayas and Andes, causing erosion of soils, siltation of rivers, recurring floods, and landslides (Holdgate *et al.* 1982, p. 214).

Most of the wood in developing countries is used for cooking and heating. Over 100 million of people in developing countries are already experiencing acute firewood shortages, and about 2.7 million will not be able to meet minimum needs on a sustainable basis by the year 2000 (Lanly 1982). For these reasons, there is an urgent need to develop alternative sources of energy for home consumption.

The depletion of tropical forests represents the most drastic destruction of habitat for *terrestrial biota*. About 1000 species of birds and mammals and 10 percent of the species of flowering plants are estimated by the IUCN to be threatened with extinction in forests and other biomes (Holdgate *et al.* 1982, p. 216). Apart from esthetic and ethical considerations of the elimination of our "contemporary life companions on this planet" (Mueller-Dombois *et al.* 1983, p. 1), the loss of potentially valuable genetic resources should not be shrugged off in favour of short-term gains from land and water development. The valuation of genetic resources is difficult and has been considered speculative, which is probably the reason for the relatively low priorities assigned to the conservation of these resources (see Table 2.1, above). Surprises in the usefulness of wild plants and animals have been, and will continue to be, experienced in such fields as medicine, food, pest control, and the restoration of ecosystems (Mueller-Dombois *et al.* 1983, p. 6 *et seq.*). The preservation of genetic resources is thus one of the principal objectives of the World Conservation Strategy (see Table 3.3, below).

Energy consumption per capita is an indicator of the large difference in the level of economic development of countries. In 1979, developed market economies consumed about 13 times as much energy per person as developing market economies. Despite their relatively low level of energy consumption, developing countries are vulnerable to energy price fluctuations, as provoked by the recent oil crises, since they spend between 25 percent and 65 percent

Plate 2.1 Desertification caused by overgrazing at the Sahara's fringe in western Sudan. (*Source*: Mark Edwards/Earthscan.)

Plate 2.2 Use of stagnant rainwater (Colombia).
(*Source*: German Castro/Earthscan.)

Plate 2.3 Forest burnt for farming in western Brazil.
(*Source*: Marcos Santilli/Earthscan.)

Plate 2.4 Carrying fuelwood (Niger). (*Source*: Mark Edwards/Earthscan.)

Plate 2.5 Drought victim (Sudan). (*Source*: Mark Edwards/Earthscan.)

Plate 2.6 Shanty town in Tehran. (*Source*: Sean Sprague/Earthscan.)

Plate 2.7   River blindness (Burkina Faso). (*Source*: UN photo.)

Plate 2.8   Sea-bed mining: manganese nodules. (*Source*: UN photo.)

Table 2.5 Proved recoverable fossil-fuel reserves and potentials of other energy sources.

	Coal and peat (%)	Oil (1979) (%)	Natural gas (1979) (%)	Hydropower (1978)		Coastline wind (potential) (%)
				Potential annual output[a] (%)	Potential output harnessed[b] (%)	
Africa	4.7	9	9.9	26.2	(4.3)	10.9
Asia	16.7					14.2
– Far East/Pacific		3	4.5	25.1	(22.0)	
– Middle East		57	27.7			
Latin America		9	6.3	14.7	(27.2)	12.3
other	78.6	22	50.6	34.0	(–)	62.6
world total	100.0	100	100.0	100.0	(35.1)	100.0

Source: Holdgate *et al.* (1982, p. 460 *et seq.*).

[a] Potential electricity production from installed and installable generating capacity at 50% capacity factor.
[b] Current annual production as a percentage of potential annual output.
[c] Not available separately, but included in world total.

of their foreign currency earnings on oil imports (Holdgate *et al.* 1982, p. 454). On the other hand, the quadrupling of oil prices between 1973 and 1979 may have prevented the total exhaustion of recoverable oil reserves by the end of the century. The 14 percent drop in world oil consumption between 1979 and 1983 is largely due to reduced consumption by Western industrialized countries and Japan. Some developing countries succeeded in substituting other energy sources, such as hydropower or alcohol, for petroleum; others continue to increase their consumption of oil (Brown *et al.* 1984, pp. 35–43).

Table 2.5 gives estimates of some energy reserves in major regions, which may affect future trends of energy consumption. In many cases, the exploitation of these reserves will produce serious environmental impacts. Coal seems to be a promising source of energy in Asia, but mining the resource may degrade land and create problems of water pollution. The table also shows the concentration of oil and gas reserves in the Middle East, the exploitation of which entails hazards of air and marine pollution for the region. A high-potential energy source for developing countries is hydropower, especially in Africa. Typical environmental impacts of hydropower development are the displacement of settlements, the disruption of river ecosystems and the spread of water-borne diseases. The development of wind power seems to be an important source of future energy, though somewhat limited – largely to development along coastlines.

In the mid-seventies, nuclear-power programs were initiated with great hopes by 16 developing countries. As of mid-1983, however, only six countries had a total of 13 operating nuclear plants. This development reflects, besides technical problems of safety and waste disposal, the lack of competitiveness of nuclear power as compared with other, cheaper sources of energy (Brown *et al.* 1984, pp. 115–35). Other significant environmental impacts of energy production and use stem from the reliance of many developing nations on fuelwood, charcoal, crop waste and

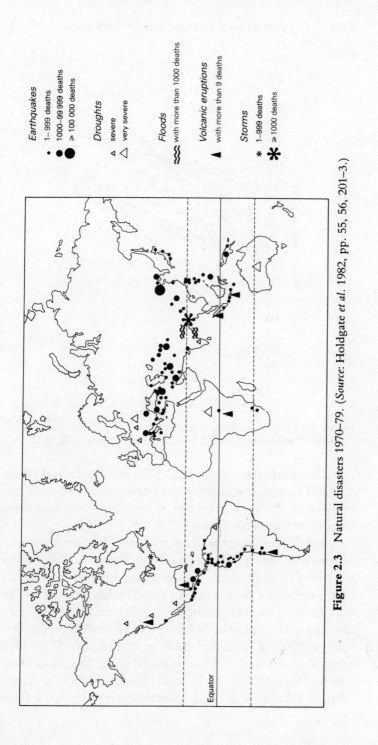

Figure 2.3 Natural disasters 1970–79. (*Source:* Holdgate *et al.* 1982, pp. 55, 56, 201–3.)

Earthquakes
· 1–999 deaths
•● 1000–99 999 deaths
● ≥ 100 000 deaths

Droughts
△ severe
△ very severe

Floods
〰 with more than 1000 deaths

Volcanic eruptions
▲ with more than 9 deaths

Storms
∗ 1–999 deaths
✳ ≥ 1000 deaths

Equator

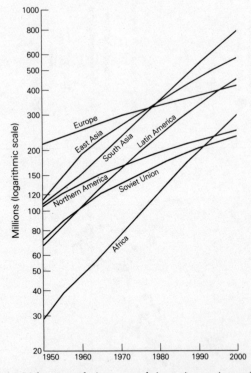

Figure 2.4 Urban population growth in major regions of the world. (*Source*: Centre for Housing, Building and Planning 1976, p. 21.)

dung for domestic energy requirements. Fuelwood (Plate 2.4) and charcoal production are responsible for large-scale removal of the vegetation cover, creating desert-like areas around human settlements.

Natural events become disasters when they are the cause of losses in life, limb and property. Figure 2.3 highlights the heavy concentration of such disastrous events in developing countries during the 1970s. The highest toll in life was taken by the Tangshang earthquakes of July 1976, with an estimated number of 242 000 people killed. Over 200 000 lives were lost in Bangladesh in November 1970 in a tropical storm combined with a tidal bore. The continuing extreme droughts of the Sudano-Sahelian region in Africa (Plate 2.5) have accelerated desertification processes and are responsible for hunger and death in the region. In the case of floods, much of the increases in frequency and intensity of occurrence can be ascribed to human activities, such as the upstream deforestation in the Himalayas mentioned above.

Human settlements consist of the physical elements – shelter and infrastructure – and of community services such as education, health, culture, welfare, recreation and nutrition (United Nations 1976, p. 37). In developing countries, the lack of or the low quality of both the physical and the non-material components of human settlements are an illustration of how poverty affects the quality of the environment and of living conditions. Accelerated urbanization, as illustrated by the steep slopes of urban-population growth in Africa, Asia and Latin America in Figure 2.4, is at the root of most environmental impacts on human settlements of developing nations. This process seems to be the result of natural growth of the urban population rather than of rural–urban migration (which is, however, a significant contributing factor). It is estimated that by the year 2000 developing countries will have 61 cities of more than four million inhabitants as compared with about 25 such cities in developed countries. Yet the majority of the population still lives in rural areas in developing countries (Holdgate *et al*. 1982, pp. 337 and 338).

The most serious impact of urbanization is the mushrooming of marginal settlements within and at the periphery of the large cities (Plate 2.6). It has been estimated that in developing countries about one-third of the urban population lives in overcrowded makeshift shelters which lack basic sanitation, a clean water supply, and waste-disposal facilities. These people also lack adequate services of transportation, health, education and recreation (Holdgate *et al*. 1982, p. 342). Under these conditions, crime and prostitution flourish, and communicable diseases may reach epidemic proportions. Table 2.6 shows that in some cities the population in marginal settlements may well exceed that in conventional housing.

Table 2.6 Slums and squatter settlements in selected cities.

City	Year	Total population		Population in slums and squatter settlements		
		number ('000)	annual growth rate (%)	number ('000)	annual growth rate (%)	% of total population
Addis Ababa	1966	680	5.5	612	...	90
Casablanca	1971	1506	5.7	1054	...	70
Mexico City	1966	3287	2.3	1500	12.0	46
Bogotá	1969	2294	7.3	1376	...	60
Calcutta	1971	8000	2.5	5238	9.1	67
Manila	1972	4400	4.0	1540	5.5	35

Source: Statistical Office of the Department of Economic and Social Affairs of the United Nations (1976, Table 18).

For selected cities, these statistics indicate the overall magnitude and trends of marginal settlements; they do not reveal, however, their large physical, ethnic and social diversity. Inner-city slums and peripheral squatter settlements may consist of pavement settlements, shelters constructed from sacking and packing cases and rusting sheets of corrugated iron, matting huts on arid hillsides, and settlements on steep slopes or in swamps unsafe for permanent housing. A considerable variation in the slum dwellers' perception of their own situation has also been observed. The distinction between "slums of hope" and "slums of despair" illustrates vividly attitudes that may range from aspirations for a better future to resignation to a life in squalor and poverty (Lloyd 1979, pp. 15 and 208).

Environmental diseases are those that are affected by living conditions, climate and water supply in developing countries (Plate 2.7). Average life expectancy is still considerably lower in these countries than in developed ones, but the difference is expected to narrow by the beginning of the twenty-first century (Table 2.7). Communicable and vector-borne diseases, such as respiratory diseases, malaria,

Table 2.7 Life expectancy at birth in major regions of the world.

	1975–80 (years)	2020–25 (years)
developed regions	71.9	75.4
less-developed regions	55.1	69.6
Africa	48.6	67.2
Latin America	62.5	71.8
East Asia	67.6	74.8
South Asia	50.7	68.6

Source: Holdgate *et al.* (1982, p. 361).

schistosomiasis and onchocerciasis, account for a high proportion of mortality and morbidity in developing countries. Water-development schemes, for hydropower, flood regulation and irrigation, create and spread habitats for disease vectors. Infant mortality has been considered a more sensitive indicator of social and health conditions than life expectancy because small children are especially affected by mal- and undernutrition, poor sanitation and lack of medical care (Eckholm 1977, p. 22). It is estimated that each year some five million children die from diphtheria, whooping cough, tetanus, measles, polio and tuberculosis. Motor-vehicle accidents have also become a major environmental hazard in developing countries, because of increasing traffic and lack of training and safety measures (Holdgate *et al.* 1982, pp. 358 and 500).

Some global issues

The environmental problems discussed above represent the major environmental impacts observed in developing countries. A number of environmental resources and phenomena are, however, beyond the control of national jurisdiction. These "global commons" are considered to be the common heritage and property of mankind and have thus received the particular attention of international organizations. Though international in scope and character, these issues may exert significant impacts on national environments.

Increases of *carbon-dioxide concentration* in the atmosphere, estimated at about 15 percent over the past century, have been caused by the combustion of fossil fuels and to a lesser degree by deforestation. Further increases might eventually raise average annual global surface temperatures by 2°–3°C, and possibly by 7°–10°C, in the northern polar region during winter. Such rises in temperature could change rainfall patterns and ecosystems, and might raise the sea levels because of the melting of polar icecaps (OECD 1982, pp. 8 and 9). It is not clear to what extent these impacts might be beneficial or detrimental, especially for bioproductive systems.

No distinct trend of *ozone depletion* could be detected in the atmosphere. It is feared, however, that there are still threats to the protective ozone layer from the release of chlorofluorocarbons from aerosol cans and refrigeration equipment, from nitrous oxides emitted during fuel combustion, and from denitrification of fertilizers. As a consequence, the incidence of skin cancer might increase and food crops might be damaged (Council on Environmental Quality 1980, p. 37).

Pollution by oil, sewage, chemicals and metals, depletion of whales and fish stocks, and the exploitation of mineral resources of the sea bed (Plate 2.8) are the major concerns regarding the *marine environment*. A recent international study of the incidence and distribution of oil pollution of the world's oceans found that "surface contamination in the form of slicks and floating tar was most prevalent near major tanker routes and that concentrations of dissolved/dispersed petroleum residues in the µg/liter range were present almost everywhere at a depth of one meter in the water column" (Levy 1984, p. 226). Fishing yields have increased markedly since World War II, but seemed to level off in the seventies. Total stocks of marine mammals were estimated to have decreased by over 50 percent during the century, with some species approaching extinction (Holdgate *et al.* 1982, p. 102). The United Nations Convention on the Law of the Sea (United Nations 1983b) was adopted in 1982 by the United Nations Conference on the Law of the Sea. The votes against the treaty and the abstention by a number of industrialized countries have been taken as an indication of these countries' "plans of appropriating the sea-bed resources" (Sachs 1982, p. 370).

Suggestions for further reading

International surveys of environmental problems   The *Global 2000 report* shows trends in population, natural resources and environment. Assuming no major social disruptions and changes in public policies and technological advances, the report finds that "the world in 2000 will be more crowded, more polluted, less stable ecologically and more vulnerable to disruption than the world we live in now" (Council on Environmental Quality 1980, p. 1). Simon and Kahn (1984) come to exactly the opposite conclusions in a direct critique of *Global 2000*.

The *World environment report* of UNEP takes stock of developments since the establishment of UNEP and evaluates the environmental problems that have been solved and others that have appeared. According to the report, the understanding of environmental systems and of the machinery and technology to solve environmental problems has greatly advanced, though "there was less confidence in the capacity of national and international managerial systems to apply known principles and techniques" (Holdgate *et al.* 1982, p. 630). The report reviews the state of and change in 15 areas, covering the environmental media of air, land and water, major activities affecting the environment (settlements, industry, energy and transport) and their impacts, especially on human health. A more selective report by UNEP highlights major environmental events that took place during the same (1972–82) period (El-Hinnawi & Hashmi 1982).

The Worldwatch Institute's *State of the world 1984* tries to measure progress towards the sustainability of society. The report focuses on demographic trends, energy production and consumption, soil loss, forest resources and food supplies, and comes to the conclusion that sustainability cannot be obtained if current trends continue. The need for two "transitions" is therefore stressed – "from primary dependence on fossil fuels to a reliance on renewable energy resources, and from an equilibrium of high birth and death rates to one of low birth and death rates" (Brown *et al.* 1984, p. 208).

Other international reports are regional in scope and provide further information for their respective geographical areas. For Asia and the Pacific, the status and trends of environmental conditions, and the responses of countries to these conditions, are described in a report on the *State of the environment* (UN ESCAP 1985). The *State of the environment* report of the OECD (1985) covers the industrialized market economies. It describes activities having an impact on the environment, the environmental conditions in member countries, and actions taken to alleviate stress on the environment. The instruments and challenges of environment and development in Africa are presented in a study by Environmental Development Action in the Third World (ENDA 1981).

National environmental reports   A number of developing countries began assessing the state of the national environment as a contribution to the United Nations Conference on the Human Environment in Stockholm, 1972. Since then, many other countries have prepared quantitative and qualitative descriptions of their environment. The U.S. Environmental Protection Agency has collected environmental reports and published summaries of these reports until December 1977, when this exercise was discontinued (U.S. Environmental Protection Agency 1977). U.S. AID-sponsored "Environmental Profiles" of countries are available (in draft form) from the Arid Lands Information

Center of the University of Arizona. Brief environmental profiles are given for about 100 countries in a directory of environmental agencies (Baker *et al*. 1985).

Data sources, needs and categories A recurrent lament in most of the international surveys and country reports concerns the lack of the data required for the assessment of the environment. Surveys carried out by the Statistical Office of the United Nations found that there is a great wealth of data even in developing countries. However, environmental data are dispersed and vary in quality which makes them difficult to compile and to process (United Nations 1982a). Based on these surveys, a *Directory of environment statistics* (United Nations 1983a) was issued. The *Directory* lists statistical parameters collected and published, in particular by the statistical services of countries and international organizations.

UNEP's Earthwatch programme (briefly described in UNEP 1984) has been designed to assist in the assessment of the global state and trends of the environment. It is a collaborative effort of numerous international and national, governmental and non-governmental organizations. The major components of Earthwatch are: (a) the Global Environment Monitoring System (GEMS), which focuses on the monitoring of natural resources, climatic changes, pollution and the oceans; (b) Infoterra, which is an international reference system of sources of environmental information; and (c) the International Register of Potentially Toxic Chemicals (IRPTC), which provides information for the evaluation of hazards associated with chemicals entering the environment.

The use of environmental data in various stages of the process of environmental management is described by Bartelmus (1979b). The author distinguishes between monitoring data, typically measured by monitoring stations under laboratory conditions, environment statistics, collected by statistical offices, and environmental indicators or indices, which are the result of further processing of raw statistical or monitoring data. A good example of an environmental index is the Pollution Standard Index of the USA (U.S. Federal Interagency Task Force 1976), which contains the ambient measures of 15 major air pollutants.

Natural resource inventories and baseline surveys assess the quantity and quality of natural resources and monitor ecological processes (Conant *et al*. 1983). They tend to be either too complex (in assessing specific ecosystems) or too narrow (in focusing on particular species) to catch routinely the attention of national decision-makers. Numerous examples of this limited approach to environmental data collection are given in Bell and Atterbury (1983).

3 Planning: the ecodevelopment approach

Man and ecosystem

The preceding chapter identified the major environmental concerns of developing countries. It described the degradation of natural resources in bioproductive systems, desertification, environmental impacts of energy production and consumption, natural disasters, marginal living conditions in human settlements, and environmentally conditioned diseases. Most of these problems were caused by human interaction with the environment. Problem-solving – that is planning and policy-making – requires a more rigid analysis of these interactions in their particular spatial and temporal context.

The concept of the ecosystem has been used to model the whole of interactions of populations with the non-living components of their environment in a particular area (Odum 1971, pp. 5 and 8). Figure 3.1 is a simplified model of the ecosystem, illustrating interactions as flows between living organisms and the non-living natural environment. Man and the man-made environment are introduced as a separate component to show material flows between the socioeconomic and ecological systems (flows crossing the boundaries of the socioeconomic system). Those flows that have direct influence on human welfare are shown as arrows that hit the man-circle inside the socioeconomic system (marked with a plus sign (+) for welfare increases and with a minus sign (−) for welfare impairment). For reasons of simplicity, a number of important internal processes are hidden in a "black box" in the flow chart, or neglected: these include interactions of species within communities, the role of organisms and climate in soil develop-

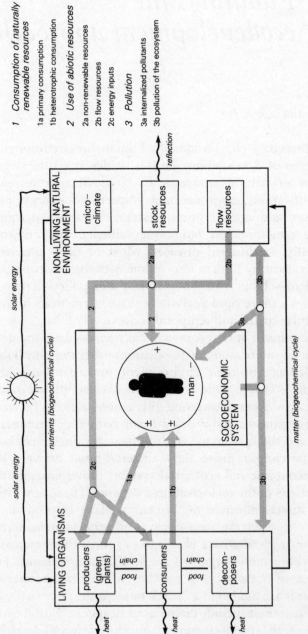

Figure 3.1 Man and ecosystem.

1 *Consumption of naturally renewable resources*
1a primary consumption
1b heterotrophic consumption

2 *Use of abiotic resources*
2a non-renewable resources
2b flow resources
2c energy inputs

3 *Pollution*
3a internalized pollutants
3b pollution of the ecosystem

ment, and human activities in their habitat. In fact, human habitat can be regarded as an ecosystem of its own, as will be shown below.

The flows of the chart reflect the fundamental functions of the human environment: resource supply (flows 1 and 2), and waste and pollutants disposal (flow 3). Flows 1a and 1b represent the human consumption of renewable resources produced by bioproductive systems. Ecological theory distinguishes between primary consumption (1a), of fruits, fibres, wood, cotton and so on, and heterotrophic consumption (1b) of herbivores and carnivores. The effects of these consumptive activities can be positive or negative for human welfare. Food and the esthetic, cultural or recreational enjoyment of nature are direct contributions of the biotic environment to human wellbeing. On the other hand, food consumption may involve intake of non-degradable chemical poisons. These chemicals are emitted as pollutants into the ecosystem (3b) and may accumulate in food chains.

Use of abiotic resources is made either from mineral deposits (non-renewable stock resources, 2a) or from tapping the constant supply of flow resources such as air and water (2b). The physiological consumption of mainly flow resources is indicated as a positive effect on man. An important energy input into bioproductive systems is shown in the figure as a throughput across the socio-economic system which molds the raw material into readily usable energy forms (2c). These energy flows can be considered as auxiliary, subsidizing man's transformation of natural growth processes by such means as mechanization, irrigation, fertilization or chemical pest control in agriculture, ranching and forestry (see below).

Ecological impacts of these activities include the reduction of ecosystem diversity by artificial selection or domestication of plants and animals. The stability of the ecosystem may thus be decreased, making it more vulnerable to pests, diseases and further human impacts. In addition, the removal of the vegetation cover by tree cutting and overgrazing creates soil degradation and erosion which in the long run impair the productivity of agriculture and forestry. For example, large-scale clearing of tropical forests for agriculture and settlement has been responsible for the breakdown of nutrient cycles and the corresponding decline of soil quality and agricultural yields.

The flow of pollutants (3) stems from productive and consumptive activities of man. Pollutants can take diverse forms such as gaseous or particulate air pollutants, pesticides, thermal and radioactive radiation, and solid and liquid wastes. Impacts on man and the socioeconomic system (3a) can be distinguished from those on ecosystems (3b). The effects of the former are brought about by the internalization of pollutants either by human beings themselves, resulting in the impairment of human health, or by the economic productive system, creating external costs (diseconomies) which disturb the optimal allocation of resources in the economy (Bartelmus 1980, p. 59 *et seq.*). In addition, corrosion of stone and metal by acidic compounds may damage artefacts of importance to man's sociocultural environment. Pollution impacts on the natural system itself may disrupt the system's biogeochemical cycles and may disturb the ability of the ecosystem to maintain its equilibrium. Pollutants may also poison plants and animals, disturb photosynthetic processes, and produce climatic changes.

In order to identify in a synoptic way man's impacts on natural ecosystems, internal relationships within the boxes of the flow chart have been neglected. The central box of man's socioeconomic system deserves some elaboration, however, because it is the ultimate target for all development efforts. It is one of the best-researched systems and has recently also attracted the attention of ecologists. The new ecosystem approach to human settlements proceeds from the fact that settlements are located in ecosystems or ecosystems in settlements (Lee-Smith 1978, p. 3). An "integrated ecological approach" to the analysis and planning of human settlement systems has been advocated, taking into account energy and materials flows through the system as well as the human biological, sociocultural, economic and psychological dimensions of the system (UNESCO 1981a, p. 9).

Natural and man-made ecosystems differ distinctly, however, in their aims and the means of achieving these aims. Human values and perceptions are expressed by social needs such as love, work or participation. The cultural, as opposed to the genetical, way of storing, transmitting and applying information also lends unique characteristics to social systems. Psychosocial needs and growing knowledge and technology together produce various forms of social behavior, ranging from aggressive through indifferent to altruistic. To some extent, these behavior patterns may be found in non-human communities, too. However, the strong supporting machinery developed by human ingenuity may produce impacts on both human and non-human systems that exceed by far nature's powers of development and destruction.

The above gives a fairly static picture of man's interaction with ecosystems. To understand the forces that resist or yield to human impacts in ecosystems one has to have some knowledge of ecosystem dynamics and in particular of the concept of ecosystem equilibrium. "Ecosystems are capable of self-maintenance and self-regulation as are their component populations and organisms" (Odum 1971, p. 33). They tend to resist change and to remain in a state of equilibrium. There are however limits to the adaptability of ecosystems. The concept of the homeostatic plateau refers to the state of an ecosystem operating within limits. Within these limits, negative-feedback (deviation-counteracting) forces keep the system in relative stability as regards the maintenance of particular sets of nutrient and energy pathways, of certain key populations — including man — and of the quality of their environment. However, positive-feedback stresses may push the system beyond the limits of the plateau, leading to its rapid deterioration and final destruction.

An important feature of ecosystem dynamics is that "really good homeostatic control for the preservation of the ecosystem comes only after a period of evolutionary adjustment" (Odum 1971, p. 35). Ecosystems typically display a strategy of development, termed "ecological succession," which culminates in a climax system of high diversity, large biomass and high stability. Such mature systems protect organisms against perturbations of the physical environment or facilitate their adaptation to environmental changes. The costs of achieving stability can be accounted for as shifts of energy flows from production to maintenance. In young systems, the rate of gross production of biomass and organic matter tends to exceed the rate of community respiration, that is the maintenance costs of the ecosystem. Mature systems on the other hand exhibit equal or near-equal rates of production and respiration. Young systems thus accumulate organic matter and biomass through high production rates. Obviously, man is interested in maintaining ecosystems in the young high-productivity state. He thus pursues a strategy of maximum production, as opposed to – and indeed conflicting with – nature's strategy of maximum protection or adaptation.

The maintenance of an ecosystem in an artificially young state of high productivity (e.g. of crops) requires large auxiliary energy subsidies in diverse forms such as fertilizers, fuels for machinery, irrigation, genetic selection or pest control. If these requirements cannot be met, productivity of agriculture in terms of harvest weight, calorie contents and dry-matter production will decrease rather than improve. Such processes have frequently taken place, especially in developing countries that attempted to mechanize agriculture without the costly energy subsidies. It is the main challenge of the new ecodevelopment concept to show how nature's strategy of ecological succession can be reconciled with man's strategy of maximum production for development. The use of environmentally sound "ecotechniques" (see below) plays a crucial role in this harmonious approach to ecosystem development.

Ecodevelopment planning

Most impacts on ecosystems stem from activities of socio-economic development. Ecological criteria need, therefore, to be introduced into development planning and policies. Ecological criteria have always been applied by traditional agrarian communities which are closely linked to the rhythm and productivity of nature. A good example of full identification of tribal communities with their physical environment and of their successful management of a well-balanced ecosystem is the hand-built rice paddy terraces on steep mountain slopes in the Philippines (World Bank 1982, p. 18). Successful management of local environments is also evidenced by swidden cultivation in tropical rainforests and traditional herd management by nomads in semi-arid zones.

Aware of these ecological successes and of the relevance of ecological factors in the development process, the new planning concept of *ecodevelopment* has been advocated, in particular by UNEP. The same organization also offered one of the first explicit definitions of ecodevelopment, as "development at regional and local levels ... consistent with the potentials of the area involved, with attention given to the adequate and rational use of the natural resources, and to applications of technological styles ... and organizational forms that respect the natural ecosystems and local sociocultural patterns" (UNEP 1975, para. 100).

This definition suggests a new "ecoregional" approach to development planning in referring explicitly to both ecological and sociocultural habitat. It is in this sense of reference to a well-defined ecoregion that the concept of ecodevelopment is used here. The term has sometimes been used, however, as a synonym for environmentally sound development, irrespective of the geographical (local, national or international) boundaries to which environmental and socioeconomic planning should apply. Riddell (1981), for example, includes in his "principles" and "desiderata" of ecodevelopment objectives such as the overall alleviation of hunger, disarmament or environmental protection, which resemble international proclamations on environment and development rather than the ecosystem- or habitat-oriented planning approach advanced here as ecodevelopment.

The concept of ecodevelopment planning was picked up on behalf of UNEP by a non-governmental organization, the Centre International de Recherche sur l'Environnement et le Développement. This organization developed numerous pilot studies and established the following main features of ecodevelopment (Sachs 1976 & 1980):

(a) resource development for the satisfaction of basic needs;
(b) development of a satisfactory social ecosystem;
(c) rational (non-degrading and non-wasteful) use of natural resources in solidarity with future generations;
(d) use of alternative environmentally sound production procedures;
(e) use of alternative energy sources, in particular of the regional capacity for photosynthesis;
(f) development and use of ecotechniques;
(g) establishment of a horizontal authority ensuring participation of the population concerned and preventing any plundering of the results of ecodevelopment;
(h) preparatory education to create social awareness of ecological values in development.

A simple model of the general planning process (Fig. 3.2) is used to analyze the role of ecodevelopment features at different planning stages. At the initial stages, when problems are identified and corresponding objectives for their solution are formulated (boxes 1 and 2 of Fig. 3.2), ecodevelopment focuses on the values and perceptions of the local population (box 0). Initially, self-reliance was advocated for the population so "that the style and rate of development ... be determined by those people most

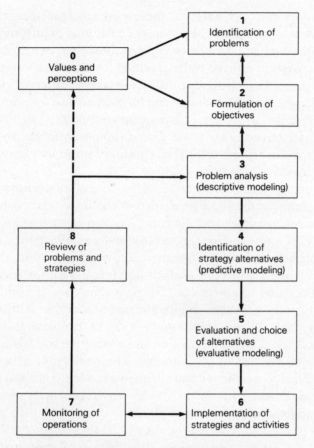

Figure 3.2 Major stages of the planning process.

affected" (UNEP 1976, p. 2). However, this approach overlooked largely the political realities of power structures, that is the dependence of local communities on "outside" institutions which control land tenure, commercial channels, and law and order. Participative planning was later proposed for the development of communication between the local population, the government and national elites. It is hoped that local "inside" institutions will emerge eventually with sufficient power to obtain a stronger bargaining position for meeting and communicating with central authorities (Billaz *et al.* 1976, pp. 28–9).

At the most general level, there is little disagreement that ecodevelopment should pursue the basic goal of improving human welfare. Conflicts emerge, however, when concrete objectives have to be specified for various groups of the population, different decision-makers, different time horizons (short-, medium- and long-term) and for various ecosystems and their components (resources, processes, and organisms). To some extent, inconsistencies can be overcome through improved communication by means of participative planning.

Further analysis is required to assess environmental problems at the local level, that is the inter-relationships between activities and their impacts and repercussions on the ecological and local economic and social systems. The figure suggests descriptive modeling for this purpose (box 3). Feedback from this analysis into box 2 is for the review and revision of objectives. The major purpose of problem analysis (box 3) is to produce information for the identification (box 4) and selection (box 5) of problem-solving strategies. Various predictive and evaluative models have been developed in this context. The distinction between descriptive, predictive and evaluative models is arbitrary to some extent. In many cases, environmental models combine characteristics of all three categories, that is of boxes 3, 4 and 5, as will be shown below.

Considerable organizational problems of coordinating between sectors, and between local, regional and national policy-making institutions have to be overcome before chosen strategies can be implemented (box 6). These issues will be addressed in Chapter 4. When implementing ecodevelopment strategies and activities, the impacts of these operations have to be monitored (box 7) for a feedback into current activities (box 6) and for a general review of problems and strategies (box 8). Such a review may give rise to a new assessment of environmental problems, thus closing the overall feedback loop of the planning process at box (3).

Table 3.1 Inter-regional economic–ecologic framework of inter-actions.

| | | | | Land | | Marine |
| | | | | Zone A | ... | Zone U | Zone A |

(A large matrix table cross-tabulating economic categories (agriculture, manufacturing, services, government) and ecologic categories (climate, geology, physiography, hydrology, soils, plants, animals) across Land Zone A, Zone U, and Marine Zone A, on both row and column dimensions. The grid cells are empty.)

Row structure (Land / Marine, Zone A ... Zone U, economic / ecologic):
- **Land — Zone A — economic:** agriculture, manufacturing, services, government
- **Land — Zone A — ecologic:** climate, geology, physiography, hydrology, soils, plants, animals
- **Land — Zone U — economic:** agriculture, manufacturing, services, government
- **Land — Zone U — ecologic:** climate, geology, physiography, hydrology, soils, plants, animals
- **Marine — Zone A — economic:** agriculture, manufacturing, services, government
- **Marine — Zone A — ecologic:** climate, geology, physiography, hydrology, soils, plants, animals

Column structure mirrors the rows: Land Zone A (economic: agriculture, manufacturing, services, government; ecologic: climate, geology, physiography, hydrology, soils, plants, animals), ... Land Zone U (economic and ecologic as above), Marine Zone A (economic: agriculture, manufacturing, services).

Source: Isard *et al.* (1972, p. 60).

Modeling ecodevelopment

Planning models deal with the assessment of problem areas, the identification of functional relationships between relevant variables and parameters, and the description, evaluation and selection of problem-solving strategies (see boxes 3–5 in Fig. 3.2). The following approaches to modeling complex inter-relationships have frequently been used for the integration of ecological with economic systems.

Interaction tables of the *input–output system* have been suggested as the appropriate framework for the description of socioeconomic and environmental inter-relationships (Walters & Peterman 1978, pp. 326–7). Table 3.1, which was designed for environmentally sound economic planning in the Plymouth Bay area of Massachusetts (Isard *et al.* 1972), is an example of an inter-regional framework of economic–ecologic interactions. Each zone of the two basic regions, land and marine, is subdivided into ecologic and economic activities. Interactions can be identified simply by earmarking relevant table fields or may be quantified in terms of physical flow or impact indicators for a specific period of time.

The identification and description of human and ecological interactions is only a first step in the planning and management process. Input–output matrices such as the one of Table 3.1 can be developed into more sophisticated models of decision-making by assuming functional linear or non-linear relationships between inputs and outputs, allowing for constraints such as environmental standards, and by introducing an objective function for the selection of an optimal strategy. Models of *activity analysis* are particularly well suited to dealing with interdependent socioeconomic and ecological processes and activities (Bartelmus 1979a). The approach of activity analysis is to determine a feasibility space of alternative activities that do not violate environmental and economic limits and to select optimal strategies according to an externally determined objective function. Table 3.2 illustrates how this approach copes with most of the ecodevelopment criteria listed above.

Activity analysis is largely a static approach with prediction restricted to externally determined changes of certain control variables, assuming constancy of – usually linear – relationships of variables. By contrast, the *system-analytic approach* views environmental problems in the broader context of the decision-making process. Dynamic features are introduced explicitly into the decision-making

Table 3.2 Activity analysis of ecoregions

Ecodevelopment criteria	Activities (choice variables)	Side conditions (standards, limits)	Objective function
1 Resource development for basic needs satisfaction	production	resource availability consumption requirements production capacities	maximum consumption levels
2 Rational management of natural resources (low-waste production on sustainable basis)	present and future production alternative (low-waste) production processes	resource availability emission standards	least-cost approach for given or projected activity levels
3 Avoidance of negative environmental impacts	production consumption alternative (environmentally sound) production and consumption processes	outer limits (environmental standards)	maximum production or consumption levels
4 Use of regional capacities of photosynthesis	production alternative production processes (resource use)	resource availability	maximum production levels
5 Development of ecotechniques	production alternative (environmentally sound) production processes	outer limits (environmental standards)	maximum production levels
6 Satisfactory social ecosystem	usually not included: list as "contingencies"!		
7 Appropriate institutional framework	usually not included, crucial for determining the objective function		
8 Formation of appropriate values and attitudes toward ecodevelopment	education information if not quantifiable, list as "contingencies"!	financial resources	maximum activity levels

Source: Bartelmus (1979a, p. 267).

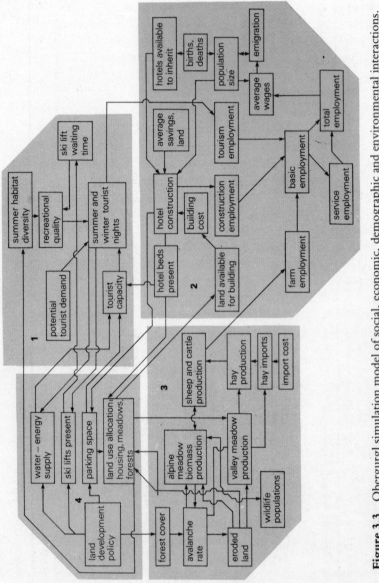

Figure 3.3 Obergurgl simulation model of social, economic, demographic and environmental interactions. (*Source:* Walters 1978.)

network by means of *simulation models*. The broad system-analytic context includes the perception of needs, problem definition, problem analysis and modeling, simulation to test alternative strategies, evaluation and selection of alternatives by decision-makers, and the implementation and monitoring of operations (Frenkiel & Goodall 1978, p. 13). Contrary to models of activity analysis, simulation models usually omit the optimization function. It has been pointed out, however, that a "good insight into the working of the environmental system" will usually provide sufficient indication of what actions should be taken (Frenkiel & Goodall 1978, p. 34). System dynamics is represented usually by large sets of difference equations.

A successful application of simulation modeling in a small ecoregion consisting of fragile ecosystems was carried out for the village of Obergurgl in the Tyrolean Alps of Austria (Walters 1978). The model resulted from a five-day workshop with active involvement of the population concerned. It produced predictions of alternative paths of long-term development, which were fully taken into consideration in the village's cooperative development efforts. Figure 3.3 shows the interactions between the four components of the model, that is recreational demand (1), population and economic development (2), farming and ecological change (3), and land use and development control (4). The environmental submodel of the third component treated three groups of phenomena, determining the status of the wild and domestic animal population, the status of forest, and changes in land use especially due to erosion processes. It was demonstrated that all processes of this submodel were relevant in the overall predictions of the model. Ecological criteria need therefore to be considered along with social and economic ones in planning for the area.

Simulation has also been advocated for the implementation of *compartment models*. The objective of compartment models is to resolve the conflict between man's strategy of exploiting high-productivity systems and nature's strategy of ecosystem maintenance by zoning the landscape into productive, protective, compromise (multiple-use), and urban-industrial environments. Starting from an intuitive or "real" model for which the flows of energy, materials and organisms are known, simulation of various zoning alternatives should help to derive "rational limits for the size and capacity of each compartment;" the intention is to achieve "a balance between use and maturity" of the social–environmental system (Odum 1971, p. 270).

Ecostrategies and ecotechniques

All the models discussed above contain elements of zoning or space management suggesting a multiple-use strategy of ecosystem management on a sustainable basis. For the implementation of this strategy, the ecodevelopment approach suggests and experiments with a variety of so-called ecotechniques.

At the international level, the World Conservation Strategy (IUCN 1980) also advocates the appropriate spatial distribution of human activities to meet three basic objectives:

(a) maintenance of essential ecological processes and life-support systems;
(b) preservation of genetic diversity;
(c) sustainable utilization of species and ecosystems.

The strategy elements listed in Table 3.3 are recommendations for action to meet these objectives. Many of the ecotechniques developed to date should be of direct use in the implementation of the strategy elements.

It is impossible, however, to describe and evaluate here all the technological experiments and solutions of ecosystem management which include diverse techniques such as:

Plate 3.1 Harambee: working together on an irrigation project in Kenya. (*Source*: Mohamed Amin/Earthscan.)

Plate 3.2 Hand-operated mill for grinding corn (Burkina Faso); the petrol-driven mill in the background has broken down. (*Source*: Colin Jones/Earthscan.)

Plate 3.3 Fish-farming Nepal. (*Source*: UN photo by Ray Witlin.)

Plate 3.4 Dune stabilization in Niger. (*Source*: Mark Edwards/Earthscan.)

Plate 3.5 Biogas production in an Indian village
(*Source*: Mark Edwards/Earthscan.)

Plate 3.6 Field terraces in an Afghan valley.
(*Source*: UN photo by Ray Witlin.)

Plate 3.7 Traditional house under construction in Niger.
(*Source*: Mark Edwards/Earthscan.)

Table 3.3 Priority requirements of the World Conservation Strategy.

	Objectives	Strategy elements
(a)	Maintenance of essential ecological processes and life-support systems	Reserve good cropland for crops; manage cropland to high, ecologically sound standards; ensure that the principal management goal for watershed forests and pastures is the protection of the watershed; ensure that the principal management goal for estuaries, mangrove swamps and other coastal wetlands and shallows critical for fisheries is the maintenance of the processes on which the fisheries depend; control the discharge of pollutants
(b)	Preservation of genetic diversity	Prevent the extinction of species; preserve as many varieties as possible of crop plants, forage plants, timber trees, livestock, animals for aquaculture, microbes and other domesticated organisms and their wild relatives; ensure that on-site preservation programs protect the wild relatives of economically valuable and other useful plants and animals and their habitats, the habitats of threatened and unique species, unique ecosystems and representative samples of ecosystem types; determine the size, distribution and management of protected areas on the basis of the needs of the ecosystems and the plant and animal communities they are intended to protect; coordinate national protected-area programs with international ones
(c)	Sustainable utilization of species and ecosystems	Determine the productive capacities of exploited species and ecosystems and ensure that utilization does not exceed those capacities; adopt conservative management objectives for the utilization of species and ecosystems; ensure that access to a resource does not exceed the resource's capacity to sustain exploitation; reduce excessive yields to sustainable levels; reduce incidental take as much as possible; equip subsistence communities to utilize resources sustainably; maintain the habitats of resource species; regulate international trade in wild plants and animals; allocate timber concessions with care and manage them to high standards; limit firewood consumption to sustainable levels; regulate the stocking of grazing lands so that the long-term productivity of plants and animals can be maintained; utilize indigenous wild herbivores, alone or in combination with livestock, where the use of domestic stock alone will degrade the land

Source: IUCN (1980).

(a) detritus agriculture;
(b) biological pest conrol;
(c) photosynthetic conversion of light;
(d) aquaculture;
(e) non-waste technology including recycling;
(f) renewable non-conventional energy sources such as biogas, sun and wind;
(g) ecodwelling;
(h) traditional medicine.

Additional information on these technologies is provided in the suggestions for further reading. Plates 3.1–7 illustrate a few examples of successfully applied ecotechniques.

An interesting notion has emerged from the development of ecotechniques, namely the concept of *combined technology* (Billaz *et al.* 1976, p. 25). The idea of applying combined technology is to make best and, if possible, integrated use of sophisticated modern innovation and traditional knowledge of the local population. An example is the integrated rural-development unit which has been successfully applied in villages in Papua New Guinea (Chan 1973). It is based on the water–waste–fuel–food cycle as exhibited in Figure 3.4. A digester treats all human and animal wastes, producing methane gas as the major fuel for domestic and small-scale industrial use. Further treatment in various ponds allows the production of feeding material for fish, ducks and crustacens. The final mineral-rich effluent is used for irrigation and fertilization of associated horticulture. The approach attempts to reinforce nature's nutrient cycles. As a result, pollution is avoided, food is supplied at low cost throughout the year, pathogenic micro-organisms are destroyed, and fuel is provided for industrialization.

Suggestions for further reading

Ecology, ecosystems and human intervention   A comprehensive and classic introduction into the "fundamentals of

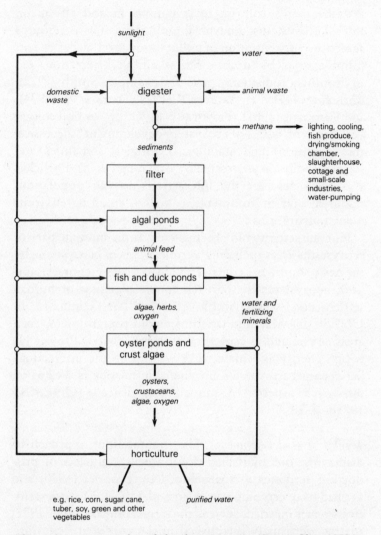

Figure 3.4 Integrated rural-development unit. (*Source*: Chan 1972.)

ecology" and the principles and concepts of ecosystems is given by Odum (1971). A more concise description is provided by Pringle (1971). Other standard textbooks on ecology, for example Colinvaux (1973), McNaughton and Wolf (1973) and Collier *et al.* (1973), also illustrate the functioning of ecosystems. Publications on human ecology describe man's role in, interventions in and effects on natural ecosystems. They deal with such issues as resource depletion, concentration of pollutants in food webs, system simplification by domestication and hybridization and environmental diseases – see, for example, Smith (1972), Ehrlich *et al*. (1973), Sargent II (1974), Turk *et al*. (1974), and Clapham (1981). Practically all textbooks on ecology deal also with issues of ecosystem development (succession and evolution) and stability. Ecological dynamics and societal evolution are treated by Boulding (1978). Ehrlich *et al*. (1977) describe the interactions among population, resources and environment, as well as resulting environmental disruptions.

Human settlements are analyzed as an integral part of ecosystems or as including various types of ecosystems by the new, somewhat controversial (regarding its practicability), ecosystematic approach to the planning of human settlements – Lee-Smith (1978). The emphasis of UNESCO's Man and the Biosphere Programme "Urban areas considered as ecological systems" (MAB Project 11) is on "energy and material flows and on the interactions between urban systems and their hinterlands as well as on intangible aspects of human experience" (UNESCO 1981b, p. 22).

Models of ecodevelopment   The input–output approach to displaying and analyzing environmental impacts of production activities was developed by Leontief (1970) and applied to an ecoregion by Isard *et al*. (1972). More descriptive impact matrices such as the pioneering Leopold (1971) matrix are usually established in the context of environmental impact assessment; an overview of the well-developed methodology of impact assessment is given by Munn (1979). Activity analysis for regional management of residuals and environmental quality has been discussed extensively by the scientists of Resources for the Future, e.g. Spofford (1973) and Russel *et al*. (1974). Environmental simulation models, including case studies and national experiences, are described by Frenkiel and Goodall (1978). General overviews on ecological modeling and simulation are given by Ott (1976) and Jorgensen (1979). Complex computerized models are listed in a register of the German Umweltbundesamt (1978).

Ecotechniques Numerous ectoechniques are described in the *Ecodevelopment News* (*Cahiers de l'Ecodéveloppement*) of the Centre International de Recherche sur l'Environnement et le Développement and in an overview by Baczko *et al.* (1977). UNEP (1979) lists environmentally sound and appropriate techniques in a volume of its Reference Series. The role of such technology in development is analyzed by Reddy (1979). Environmentally sound technologies will also be found in the vast literature on appropriate technology – see for example a bibliographic listing for developing countries (U.S. Department of Commerce 1983); Carr (1978), with specific regard to African women; Morgan and Icerman (1981), on renewable-resource use; or UNIDO (1979), dealing with the role of appropriate technology in industrial development. Ruddle and Manshard (1981) describe the application of ecologically sound technologies to the management of renewable resources.

More specifically and in direct reference to the techniques enumerated in the text, the following selected reading is suggested.

DETRITUS AGRICULTURE Cornell University (1974) and UNEP and FAO (1977) deal with the management and recycling of agricultural waste. Of particular interest is the Chinese experience: FAO (1978) or McGarry and Stainforth (1978).

BIOLOGICAL PEST CONTROL See e.g. Huffaker (1971), Ehrlich *et al.* (1973), Van den Bosch and Messenger (1973), and Delucchi (1976). A cooperative program on integrated pest control has been launched by FAO and UNEP (1975). The "ecosystem approach to integrated pest management program planning" is described by Weatherly (1983).

PHOTOSYNTHETIC CONVERSION OF LIGHT   Potentials and restrictions in the environmental and biological control of photosynthetic production are examined by Cooper (1975) and Marcelle (1975). The processes of photosynthesis and bioconversion are described by Broda (1984).

AQUACULTURE   Simple acquacultural technologies to increase world protein production are described by Bell and Canterbery (1976). The role of aquaculture in ecodevelopment is analyzed by Morales (1978). A new genetic approach to saline culture of crops is being developed by American scientists (Epstein *et al.* 1980). Neal (1984) observes an increasing role of aquaculture in food production, accompanied, however, by a growing impact on the environment.

NON-WASTE TECHNOLOGY, INCLUDING RECYCLING   Reviewed by the Royal Society of Canada (1974), Porteous (1977), UN/ECE (1978) and Barton (1979).

RENEWABLE NON-CONVENTIONAL ENERGY SOURCES   Many publications deal with renewable or alternative sources of energy. General overviews are given by the National Academy of Sciences (1976), the Commonwealth Science Council (1977), Sorensen (1979), and El-Hinnawi (1981). Various technologies and uses of non-conventional energy can be found in Furlan *et al.* (1984). The Chinese experience with the large-scale use of biogas as a solution to the energy problems in rural areas is reviewed in UNEP (1982, pp. 370–4). Brown *et al.* (1984, pp. 136–56) assess the global capacity and use of renewable energy. Weber (1982) is a source of references (with abstracts) on alternative energy sources.

ECODWELLING   Ecodevelopment and habitat design are assessed by Baczko *et al.* (1977) and by Schneier and Vinaver (1979). Some "radical" technology for shelter is suggested by Boyle and Harper (1976).

TRADITIONAL MEDICINE   The development of primary

health care using traditional medical experience is advocated by WHO (1978). Preventive instead of curative medicine, in particular in the context of environmental management, is proposed by Sigal (1979).

Good examples of successfully applied traditional ecotechniques are the sawah system of flooded paddy and the swidden agriculture in tropical forests. The Conuco system of the Waika in the upper Orinoco rainforest in Venezuela is a good demonstration of the latter (Harris 1971). The system is a seemingly disorderly polyculture which reproduces in a simplified way the original ecosystem (Romanini 1974). An overview of literature on swiddening is given by Montgomery *et al*. (1977).

4 Policy and administration: implementing ecodevelopment

Development planning – an illusion?

"Divorce between what is planned and what actually takes place is rather a common feature among developing countries" (Abdalla 1977, p. 157). This blunt statement about the outcomes of development planning reflects a widespread concern about the efficacy of currently applied models of development. As outlined in the first chapter and its reading suggestions, much of this concern stems from the difficulties in overcoming structural inequities and imbalances within countries but particularly so in international economic relations. The near-chaotic disorder in currency and capital markets, in international debt and trade and international financial flows produced its heaviest impact on the weakest and poorest economies (United Nations 1984, p. 3). As long as inequality, domination, dependence, narrow self-interest and segmentation are not replaced by equity, sovereign equality, interdependence, common interest and cooperation among nations, as featured by the New International Economic Order (United Nations 1982b, p. 3), the outlook is grim for the success of the current approaches to national development planning.

The widening gap of income and wealth between rich and poor countries does indeed point to a failure of development policies. Despite a recovery of some industrialized countries from the 1980–82 recession, development has been diagnosed to be "deadlocked" for other countries. In

1983–84, most developing countries face "lower living standards, massive unemployment and political destabilization" (United Nations 1984, p. 11).

In addition to international structural obstacles to successful development planning, concern about the efficiency of internal development planning and management has also been expressed (United Nations 1984, p. 15). The following are well-known reasons for typical plan failures (Todaro 1977, pp. 376–8, or Seers 1983, pp. 91–129):

(a) overambitious plan objectives;
(b) ignorance or neglect of conflicts between objectives;
(c) insufficiency of the database for plan design, monitoring and evaluation;
(d) lack of qualified personnel to design and carry out plans;
(e) inaccurate and inconsistent plans (due to data gaps, neglect of conflicting objectives and a lack of qualified planners);
(f) lack of communication between planning agencies, day-to-day decision-makers and those affected by decision-making;
(g) lack of political will to carry out the plan.

In various instances, unexpected events such as the sudden deterioration of terms of trade, natural disasters or political upheaval have contributed to or brought about plan failures.

All these factors may have played a role in the production of "ivory-tower plans" (Islam and Henault 1979, p. 257) which never had a chance to be implemented the way they were designed. A number of "new" approaches, strategies and principles have been offered, especially in the international discussion (see Chapter 1), for improving plan performance. They usually assign flowery attributes to planning and management such as "integrative," "alternative" or "sustainable." However, they rarely provide detailed explanations, models or guidance for the design of plans and their administration.

No attempt is made here to add to the "intellectual anarchy in development planning" (Jolly 1977, p. 31) by suggesting a few more attributes or principles from the perspective of environmental planning. Rather, a few possibilities are pointed out of where and how environmental criteria might be injected into the established planning structure and how locally applied ecodevelopment might be linked to this structure. It is to be hoped that a generally acceptable planning framework will evolve from the experience gained in merging ecodevelopment with particular planning systems.

Environmental dimensions of central plans and programs

The traditional and popular approach to socioeconomic development is the establishment of a national medium-term development plan for a period of four or five years. The plan commonly specifies the major societal objectives and indicates how they can be achieved at various planning levels. Central planning agencies typically prepare the plan in a top-down approach which distinguishes comprehensive or aggregate plans for the whole nation from sectoral and regional programs and project development. Project development is supposed to translate the overall plan into concrete developmental action (Banskota 1979, p. 320). Since this approach is still much in use in developing countries, the possibilities of introducing environmental dimensions into this planning system are examined below.

Aggregate plans Aggregate plans focus on macroeconomic variables such as national product, saving, investment, consumption and their relationships in order to stimulate the growth of national income and its distribution. As pointed out in the first chapter, the need for a broader approach to development, including non-economic goals such as environmental conservation, has now become a widely accepted principle. However, the short-sighted view of medium-term plans into only about five years ahead has been the principal obstacle to the effective integration of the environment into the national concerns and objectives. Although some symptoms of environmental degradation and depletion, as well as restoration, do appear during such a time span, many environmental and related health effects of present activities will only be felt by future generations. However, short-lived administrations cannot be expected to be overly concerned with situations that lie beyond the next few legislative periods. Such an attitude has led to what has been aptly termed "colonizing the future" (Kothari 1980, pp. 435–6). Another more practical reason for ignoring longer-term perspectives and even medium-term effects in present-day planning is the lack of operational variables and indicators which monitor the achievement of non-economic goals.

It is no surprise, therefore, that by and large only lip-service has been paid to the "integrated approach to environment and development" in most development plans. Environmental objectives are simply added to the list of plan objectives without follow-up during plan implementation. An example is the development plans of Kenya, which contain the objective of conservation of the natural and sociocultural environment; it has been contended, however, that this objective ranks well below other objectives such as economic growth, education, health and employment (Bartelmus 1980, p. 45). Such *pro forma* integration becomes evident when the compatibility of objectives is examined and conflicts among the objectives are exposed. In the case of environment, conflicts may appear as scarcities of the natural resource base of economic development or as direct environmental hazards to the wellbeing of the population. The term "outer limits" has been used to describe environmental restrictions to development objectives (see above, Chapter 1). This concept is of little help, however, unless some means is found of assessing the limits.

It remains to be seen to what extent environmental

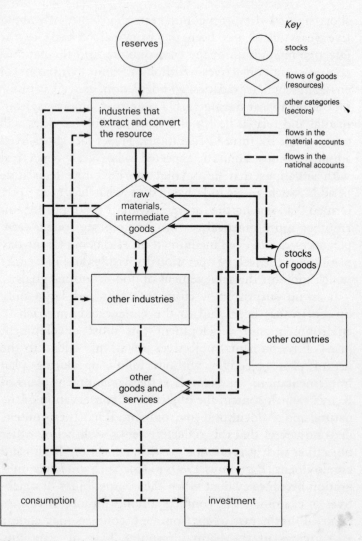

Figure 4.1 Relationships between material and national accounts. (*Source*: Statistisk Sentralbyrå 1981, p. 32.)

accounting or the narrower approach of resource accounting will produce meaningful and readily available indicators which can be related directly to the traditional economic and demographic macrodata. Figure 4.1 indicates how resource (material) accounting can be linked theoretically to national (social) accounting in terms of overlapping monetary and physical flows. Considerable problems of data collection, as well as the still unresolved issue of aggregating physical resource flows, have so far thwarted comprehensive accounting for all natural resources. Environmental accounts that purport to produce aggregate indicators of environmental quality are even more problematic. It is doubtful whether they will ever become a standard tool of environmental assessment and planning.

Sectoral programs and regional planning Sectoral programing is the intermediate stage between the establishment of societal goals and policies and their translation into actions or projects. It is usually organized in association with the major governmental departments which compete for resources to be allocated through aggregate planning. Sometimes, sectoral models such as input–output analyses are used to split up projected macro-indicators into sectoral targets. Agriculture, industry, transportation and communication, energy, health, housing, culture and security (defense) are typical sectors of government programs.

The environment is rarely treated as a separate sector in developing countries because of the interface of environmental problems with practically all planning areas. In some cases, coordinating mechanisms such as environmental agencies and secretariats or interdepartmental commissions have been established (Environmental Coordinating Unit, ESCAP 1980, p. 295 *et seq.*; Lowry & Carpenter 1984). In general, inter-sectoral coordination is quite undeveloped because data gaps and institutional barriers and jealousies prevent interdepartmental cooperation and the application of multi-sector modeling. As a consequence, allowance is rarely made within sectors for environmental programs. Rather, priority is given to sector-specific targets and projects, largely neglecting the general goals of aggregate plans.

Regional – in particular regional physical – planning has

mainly served to coordinate the implementation of sectoral programs and projects. Where programs and projects compete for space and the use of natural resources, some environmental problems become apparent as regional scarcities. The inclusion of "environmental analysis" (through regional surveys of natural resources and eco-systems) in designing regional development has, therefore, been recommended (OAS 1984). However, if environmental criteria have not been incorporated in aggregate planning or sectoral programing, environmental analysis will hardly be translated into environmental action at the project level.

Project development The identification and selection of large-scale projects to meet sectoral targets is widely considered as the principal instrument of central plan implementation. For this purpose, project planning focuses on the technological alternatives available within sectoral budgetary constraints. At the project level, environmental concerns have emerged again in view of conspicuous ecological impacts of large projects. These impacts have frequently jeopardized the project success in the medium and long run. For example, it has been estimated that the construction of the Pa Mong dam (which is part of one of the largest development programs in Asia, the Mekong project) will necessitate the resettlement of between 200000 and 500000 people, change social, economic and cultural structures of downstream rural populations, accelerate urbanization, spread malaria and schistosomiasis, produce sedimentation, create geological hazards, and affect water and soil quality, fisheries, forests and wildlife (Pantulu 1982).

One of the first reflections of this new awareness of environmental impacts of development projects are the *Environmental, health and human ecologic considerations in economic development projects* established by the World Bank as early as 1973. In developed countries, similar questions were raised. Especially for governmental activities, the preparation of environmental impact statements by means of *environmental impact assessment* (EIA) was suggested and sometimes even made mandatory. EIA has been defined as "an activity designed to identify, predict, interpret, and communicate information about the impact of an action on man's health and wellbeing (including the wellbeing of ecosystems on which man's survival depends)" (Munn 1975, p. 3). Various techniques such as checklists, matrices, overlay mapping and networking have been applied in the preparation of such environmental assessments in both developed and developing countries. The following components are typically included in a standard environmental impact statement (Munn 1975, p. 13):

(a) a description of the proposed action and alternatives;
(b) a prediction of the nature and magnitude of environment effects (both positive and negative);
(c) an identification of human concerns;
(d) a listing of impact indicators as well as the methods used to determine their scale of magnitude and relative weights;
(e) a prediction of the magnitudes of the impact indicators and of the total impact for the project and for alternatives;
(f) recommendations for acceptance or rejection of the project, for remedial action, or for acceptance of one or more of the alternatives;
(g) recommendations for inspection procedures.

Some of the general environmental objectives are reflected in the third component (human concerns) of the above list. However, the use of these concerns in evaluating alternatives is usually not made clear.

Related to EIA, though developed quite independently, is the well-established but controversial practice of *cost–benefit analysis* (CBA) for project evaluation. The object of CBA is to add up anticipated welfare effects (the benefits) of alternative projects or programs, to discount these

Table 4.1 Cost-benefit analysis of hypothetical socioeconomic development for the Valle de San Juan (Argentina).

Categories	Present condition (US dollar)	Alternative A[a] B/C = 1.74 (US dollar)	Alternative B[b] B/C = 1.71 (US dollar)	No plan (US dollar)
PROJECT COST				
construction	–	$4 500 00	$3 565 000	–
maintenance/operations	–	$3 000 000	$1 200 000	–
flooding downstream	–	$1 500 000	$ 700 000	$1 000 000
reforestation	–	0	$ 325 000	–
historic site	–	0	$ 20 000	–
maintenance/operations	–	0	$ 700 000	–
guards for wildlife reserve	–	0	$ 620 000	–
PROJECT BENEFITS	$93 000/yr	$7 850 000	$6 100 000	–
agricultural production	$80 000/yr	$5 000 000	$3 500 000	$2 500 000
flood control	$10 000/yr	$2 000 000	$1 000 000	–
recreation	$ 1 000/yr	$ 800 000	$1 500 000	$1 000 000
commercial fisheries/wildlife	$ 2 000/yr	$ 50 000	$ 100 000	–

QUALITATIVE EFFECTS

Human health (population 20 000)				
upper 10% of population	no health problems	no health problems	no health problems	no health problems
middle 70% of population	10% malaria incidence 0% bilharzia	15% malaria incidence 10% bilharzia	10% malaria incidence 5% bilharzia	10% malaria incidence 0% bilharzia
lower 20% of population	25% malaria 50% bilharzia	30% malaria 50% bilharzia	30% malaria 55% bilharzia	25% malaria 50% bilharzia
Cultural heritage	1 temple and prehistoric living site (visited by 200/yr)	flooded and destroyed	protected (visited by 10 000/yr)	1 temple and prehistoric living site deteriorating due to vandalism
Natural resources				
aquatic ecosystem	100 ha, encroached by man	flooded	protected	deteriorating due to encroachment of man
fauna (rare musk otter)	25 breeding pairs (extensive poaching)	0 breeding pairs	sustained yield (200 breeding pairs)	eventually lost

Source: OAS (1978, pp. 40–2 (consolidated)).

[a] Alternative A: Raise height of existing dam by 5 meters and build canal from existing reservoir to supply secure source of irrigation water to 15 000 hectares of cropland. Provide for full control of river.

[b] Alternative B: Extend existing canal 10 kilometers and build additional small-scale diversions to provide sufficient secure water for 9000 hectares of cropland and water that is secure for 85 percent of all years on record for an additional 7000 hectares. Include the maintenance of a unique prehistoric dwelling site and riverine ecosystem that would be flooded by increasing the reservoir area; plan for floodplain zoning and a reforestation project upstream to control flooding.

effects to their present value and to compare this value with the total project costs. The cost–benefit ratios of the alternatives are then used as criteria of project selection. Project selection is a major objective of EIA also. However, EIA does not generally attempt a monetary evaluation of impacts, in recognition of the predominantly non-economic (non-market-related) physical aspects of environmental effects. CBA on the other hand proposes to evaluate environmental impacts monetarily as far as possible, listing non-quantifiable impacts as contingencies. The controversy around CBA lies in this attempt "to price the priceless" (Schumacher 1973, p. 43), that is to put monetary values on phenomena that are not part of the monetary exchange system but that may well be more significant than the marketed project inputs and outputs.

The hypothetical example of Table 4.1 simply lists the expected costs and benefits (without attempting to discount them) of two alternative strategies of water development and control in an Argentine valley. The two strategies intend either to raise the production of horticulture crops by 40 percent and to decrease flooding costs by 20 percent (alternative A), or to maintain rare, endangered or economic species and to conserve the historic and cultural patrimony of the area at the expense of agricultural production (alternative B). The example reveals the ambiguity of these evaluations. While alternative A appears to be preferable to alternative B in obtaining a higher benefit–cost ratio (B/C) but inferior as to its qualitative effects, the no-plan situation produces a higher B/C (of 3.5) and better health conditions than either of these alternatives. It creates, however, considerable environmental degradations which have still to be accounted for.

All the above approaches to project planning reflect growing concern about environmental issues in development planning. However they are piecemeal in the sense that they fail to integrate fully national environmental values and objectives at the project level; they also fail to link project impacts to other projects and programs of the economy. There is no harmonized, that is non-conflicting, breakdown of national objectives into sectoral targets and hence into criteria of project design and evaluation. Moreover, the ability and willingness of central planners to formulate objectives and design activities that include an assessment of impacts on local ecosystems and that cater for the needs of the population living in these ecosystems may be questioned (Islam & Henault 1979, p. 257).

Decentralization: integrating ecodevelopment

The neglect of local interests in planning and plan implementation by central authorities is the major reason for the suspicion with which governmental projects and programs have been met at the grass-roots level. Too often, the benefits of such programs have never reached those levels, but have been absorbed by the wealthy and powerful in the country or region. A policy of "selective spatial closure" which would retain regional control of commodity and factor transfers to and from the region has therefore been proposed for less-developed areas (Stöhr 1981, pp. 45 and 46).

The top-down approach to development planning and policies has usually ignored the considerable knowledge of the indigenous population about local bioproductive systems. The ecodevelopment approach seeks to exploit this traditional knowledge and technology. It also emphasizes the need to account for the preferences of the population by encouraging their participation in the planning process, that is in the design and implementation of projects and programs, in the monitoring of project performance, and in the distribution of project benefits.

To achieve such participative planning, some of the authority of central government has to be delegated to local organizations. Central agencies also have to prove their willingness to learn from and support local experience. The term "decentralized planning" has been coined for this

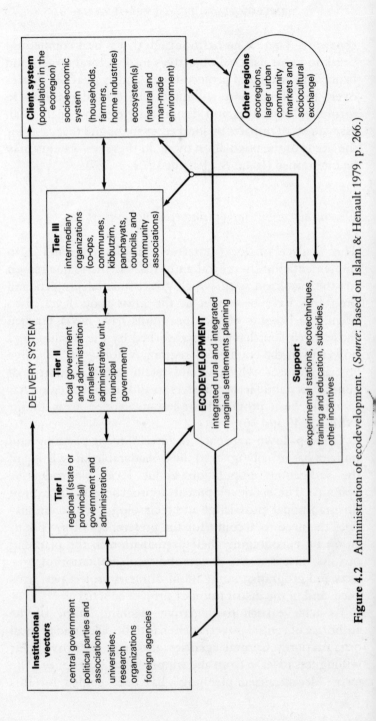

Figure 4.2 Administration of ecodevelopment. (*Source:* Based on Islam & Henault 1979, p. 266.)

bottom-up approach (Islam & Henault 1979). Decentralized planning has focused on the rural people in developing countries. "Local-level planning for integrated rural development" is a relatively new approach to encourage the participation of the rural poor in formulating and implementing development projects and activities. This approach seeks to identify and meet the needs and aspirations of the rural population and better to exploit the resource potentials of local areas (United Nations Asian Pacific Development Institute 1980, p. 193).

Local planning cannot replace central planning. Complex large-scale capital-intensive projects which may span various regions and ecosystems require central design and control. However, to the extent that such activities affect local conditions, the population and organizations in the region should also become involved in these activities. In turn, central guidance and control is needed to apply national standards to the region. These standards may relate to the distribution of income, wealth and power and to the quality of the environment.

In the process of decentralization, effective channels of communication have to be created between all planning levels (central, intermediate and local), and between organizations at the same levels. For integrated rural development planning, a "multiple-tier system" has been suggested (Islam and Henault 1979, p. 265). Figure 4.2 shows how such a system can be expanded for the implementation of ecodevelopment by including urban communities in a broader approach to the "client system" and by referring this system to an ecoregion. The client system is thus defined as the population living in an ecoregion. The figure illustrates how the multiple-tier system links the institutional vectors of the central bureaucracy through three tiers of regional and local governmental field staff and intermediary organizations of the local population to the people ("clients") in rural and urban communities in ecoregions.

Administration of ecodevelopment

The administration of ecodevelopment should be established in the crucial intermediary tier III. National environmental (and other) objectives, complex technologies, large-scale projects and the support system of information, training and financial incentives should be delivered by field staff of national and local government down to the intermediary tier of the local organizations or, where appropriate, to the client system directly. The major task of the local organizations is to facilitate the participation of the people in the planning, implementation and supervision of ecodevelopment programs and the distribution of their benefits. These organizations should build on existing formal and informal groups or associations of groups and should be of a multi-purpose nature, since they would be responsible for the whole development in the ecoregion. In the case of rural development, successful examples of such organizations are China's communes and the kibbutzim of Israel (Omer 1980, pp. 125–30).

The tier of intermediary organizations is the place for vertical communication – from the top by governmental authorities which would supervise the local organizations for understanding the "big picture," and from below by the client system which would cooperate directly with the local organizations and watch over their performance (Khan 1980, p. 68). The intermediary organizations should be in a position to mediate between those above and below, negotiating an agreement about the application of ecotechniques to the region and about monitoring local impacts of large inter-regional projects. They would be confronted with the values, ideas, needs and knowledge of the local population and could convey those to the aggregative planning process for integrated national environment and development planning.

Frequent reference has been made to local or regional areas and communities. It may be difficult, however, to determine the ideal area to which ecodevelopment should apply and which should be administered by the respective intermediary organization. In principle, such an *ecoregion* should be a homogeneous area of one or more ecosystems that interact with relatively self-contained human activities. "Self-contained" means that all major economic, social and cultural activities originate in and affect the respective ecoregion, while impacts from and to outside are minimal or are the clear responsibility of central government planning and administration.

Established criteria of a political, administrative, tribal or cultural nature might compel planners to deviate from theoretically desirable ecoregion boundaries. For example, the only politically feasible solution might be to set up a compromise region from the smallest administrative units. This procedure would introduce a certain degree of economic, cultural and ecological heterogeneity into the region. A way to enhance economic and administrative homogeneity of local areas might be the policy of selective regional closure mentioned above. Temporary economic protection of the area could provide incentives for self-reliant development and would encourage the formation of independent local organizations (Lo & Salih 1981, p. 148). Ecological heterogeneity in the form of arbitrary crossing of ecosystems by administrative boundaries would however persist.

An even greater heterogeneity has to be faced if ecodevelopment is to be applied to large urban areas. Such areas are usually not self-contained at all, but depend heavily (with the help of a large-scale, capital-intensive infrastructure) on resource flows from the hinterland and far-off regions within and even outside national boundaries. It is doubtful, therefore, whether any decentralized ecodevelopment planning and administration could and should be applied to big urban agglomerations. It remains to be seen to what extent any "integrative approaches which consider urban areas as ecosystems" (UNESCO 1981b, pp. 22–4; see also above, Chapter 3) can be successfully applied.

There are, however, relatively self-contained localities

within the large urban area. Slums and squatter settlements have usually been considered as a cancerous outgrowth of the large community, and the general policy has been to remove marginal settlements as fast and radically as possible. Slum clearance schemes failed, however, in most cases because the slum dwellers merely built new settlements in less conspicuous areas. Efforts to rehouse the displaced persons did not produce the desired results either; housing standards and costs were usually so high that the poorest members of the population could not afford the new houses (Lloyd 1979, p. 210). When not upset by such ill-conceived eradication schemes, slums and squatter settlements have coexisted with their wealthier surroundings or neighboring communities without affecting them (apart from the esthetical point of view) and without being affected. In this case, a lot of ingenuity was shown by slum dwellers, comparable to that of traditional rural life-styles. Thus, the prerequisites for the application of ecodevelopment in marginal settlements – namely self-containment of an area, failure in management of or lack of care for the area by the authorities, and substantial indigenous knowledge – are all present. Integrated planning, implementation and management of marginal settlements with the participation of their residents has therefore been suggested (Shubert 1982, pp. 259–75).

Other people at the margin of society have also been the target of ill-conceived development. Non-acculturated tribal peoples have suffered decimation or even extinction by mere contact with outside "civilizations" or through direct measures of coercion such as expropriation. As these peoples typically form an integral part of their natural habitat, they appear to practice ecodevelopment with an understanding of the human–ecological inter-relationship vastly superior to that of the intruding outsiders (World Bank 1982). The logical approach to these well-managed tribal ecoregions is probably no approach at all, unless some degree of adaptation is desired by the tribal populations themselves, and then at their own pace. Only after some acculturation has occurred might ecodevelopment of the kind described above be instilled, gingerly, into these vulnerable human ecosystems.

It has been argued that the diversity of local "pragmatic pluralistic initiatives" might be more resilient to social change than "centralized dogmatic social reform efforts" (Stokes 1978, p. 55). In this sense, ecoregions might enjoy a social stability analogous to the ecological stability of diversified climax ecosystems. Pilot studies of ecodevelopment undertaken by UNEP and other organizations were not very successful, however, mainly because of political factors. Other pilot projects in marginal settlements appear to be more promising (Shubert 1982, pp. 262–5). An analysis of case studies of development from below found that "the major limiting factor ... seems to be fear by central (national or international) decision-making centres that they might lose control" (Stöhr 1981, p. 69). The question is how to overcome the resistance of the powerful in a country to giving up power and control in the process of implementing decentralized ecodevelopment. The history of failure of violent peasant movements suggests that a slower process of local institution building might be more successful (Korten 1980, pp. 494–5). More experience with the application of ecodevelopment in specific regional settings has to be gained in order to assess how and to what degree ecodevelopment strategies should be substituted for central development strategies.

Suggestions for further reading

Project evaluation: environmental impact assessment (EIA) and cost–benefit analysis (CBA)   An overview of the methods and tools of EIA is provided by a SCOPE report (Munn 1975). The pioneering work of EIA is the Leopold (1971) matrix. A bibliography on EIA includes, besides sources on methodological questions, literature on applications in selected countries (Clark *et al.* 1980). Cheremisinoff and

Morresi (1977) describe methods and procedures for action- and legislation-oriented environmental impact statements. Golden *et al.* (1979) describe environmental data and models for EIA, referring mainly to the situation in the USA. An example of a "questionable" (see text) *ex post* impact analysis (i.e. one performed after completion of the project) is a description of the environmental impacts of the Aswan High Dam; the analysis concludes that "some of the impacts ... have negative effects but these are over-weighed, by far, when compared with the benefits so far accrued" (United Nations 1978b, pp. 17–85). The collection of "predevelopment data" through resource inventories (see the suggestions in Chapter 2 for further reading) has been suggested as an alternative to such *ex post* analysis (Conant *et al.* 1983, pp. 6–7).

The possible role of CBA in environmental management is analyzed in a UNEP study (Ahmad 1981), which also provides a synopsis of case studies in selected industrial countries. CBA and other methods of appraisal of "non-directly productive" projects are presented by Imboden (1978). Cooper (1981) suggests a distinction between "specification techniques," referring to EIA, and "evaluation techniques," attempting to measure environmental effects on social welfare. A combination of elements of both EIA and CBA for the environmental assessment of development projects has been advocated by UNEP's regional office for Asia and the Pacific, and a test model was applied in seven countries of the region (Suriyakumaran 1980).

Case studies of ecodevelopment   The dependence of development concepts on particular cultural and institutional conditions in countries and regions has been considered the main impediment to the general acceptance of an alternative development theory (Stöhr 1981, pp. 44 and 64). It has also been maintained that "the universalism of earlier theories has now been abandoned for a plurality of approaches" (Lo & Salih 1981, p. 123). Ecodevelopment itself has been considered a "heuristic instrument" rather than a new doctrine of development planning (Sachs 1980, p. 32). Case studies seem to confirm an emerging eclecticism and pragmatism in development planning. Some studies describe the failure or need for modification of center-down strategies (Stöhr & Taylor 1981); others indicate successes in spontaneous local initiatives that had been capable of learning from errors (Korten 1980).

More specifically, in the case of ecodevelopment, UNEP embarked on two pilot projects in Iran and Colombia to test the concepts and strategies of this approach. However, none of the projects achieved its goals, due mainly to the political upheaval in Iran and a change in government in Colombia. The approach to the Colombian project is described by the Centro Internacional de Formación en Ciencias Ambientales (1978); an evaluation of the project including the reasons for its failure is given in República de Colombia (1980). Similar problems led to the suspension of an ecodevelopment project in San Salvador which was initiated by the Canadian International Development Agency.

Within its MAB project area 11 on "Urban areas considered as ecological systems," UNESCO has embarked on a number of "integrative ecological studies on human settlements." The studies are largely conceptual, but are intended to be useful for integrative planning and policy formulation (Boyden 1981, p. 92). UNEP's demonstration projects for three communities in Indonesia and one in the Philippines aim to change the life-styles of the residents of marginal settlements by an "integrated environmental and socioeconomic development programme" (Shubert 1982).

References

Abdalla, I. S. 1977. Development planning reconsidered. In *Surveys for development, a multidisciplinary approach*, J. J. Nossin (ed.), 151–67. Amsterdam: Elsevier.

Ahmad, Y. J. (ed.) 1981. *The economics of survival: the role of cost–benefit analysis in environmental decision-making*. UNEP Studies, no. 4.

Ayres, R. U. 1978. *Resources, environment and economics: applications of the materials/energy-balance principle*. New York: Wiley.

Baczko, M., J. Sachs, K. Vinaver and P. Zakrzewski 1977. *Techniques douces, habitat et société*. Paris: Editions Entente.

Baker, M., L. Bassett and A. Ellington 1985. *The world environment handbook: a directory of natural resource management agencies and non-governmental environment organizations in 145 countries*. New York: World Environment Center.

Banskota, M. 1979. Environmental management: integrated project systems. In *Readings of environmental management*. Bangkok: United Nations Asian and Pacific Development Institute.

Bartelmus, P. 1979a. Limits to development – environmental constraints of human needs satisfaction. *J. Environ. Mgmt* **9**, 255–69.

Bartelmus, P. 1979b. Environment data: a tool for environmental assessment and management in developing countries. *Proceedings of the 42nd session of the International Statistical Institute*. Bull. Int. Stat. Inst. Vol. XLVIII, Book 1, 321–40. Manila: Philippine Organizing Committee.

Bartelmus, P. 1980. *Economic development and the human environment – a study of impacts and repercussions with particular reference to Kenya*. München: Weltforum.

Barton, A. F. M. 1979. *Resource recovery and recycling*. New York: Wiley.

Bell, F. W. and E. R. Canterbery 1976. *Aquaculture for the developing countries: a feasibility study*. Cambridge: Ballinger.

Bell J. F. and T. Atterbury (eds.) 1983. *Renewable resource inventories for monitoring changes and trends: proceedings of an international conference*. Corvallis: Oregon State University.

Billaz, R., M. E. Chonchol and S. Sigal 1976. *Aspects institutionnels de l'ecodéveloppement: pédagogie du milieu et organisations paysannes*. Cahiers de l'Ecodéveloppement, no. 8. Paris: Centre International de Recherche sur l'Environnement et le Développement.

Birou, A., P.-M. Henry and J. P. Schlegel (eds.) 1977. *Towards a re-definition of development*. Oxford: Pergamon.

Boulding, K. E. 1966. The economics of the coming spaceship earth. In

Environmental quality in a growing economy, H. Jarret (ed.), 3–14. Baltimore: Hopkins.

Boulding, K. E. 1978. *Ecodynamics*. Beverly Hills: Sage.

Boyden, S. 1981. Integrated studies of cities considered as ecological systems, and the role of MAB therein. In UNESCO (1981b), 89–95.

Boyle, G. and P. Harper (eds.) 1976. *Radical technology*. New York: Pantheon.

Brandt, W. *et al.* 1980. *North–South: a programme for survival*. Report of the Independent Commission on International Development Issues. Cambridge: MIT Press.

Broda, E. 1984. Photosynthesis and bioconversion. In Furlan *et al.* (1984), 491–505.

Brown, L. R. *et al.* 1984. *State of the world 1984: a Worldwatch Institute report on progress toward a sustainable society*. New York: Norton.

Caldwell, L. K. 1972. *In defense of Earth: international protection of the biosphere*. London: Bloomington.

Canadian Hunger Foundation, Brace Research Institute 1976. *A handbook on appropriate technology*. Ottawa.

Carr, M. 1978. *Appropriate technology for African women*. Addis Ababa: United Nations.

Carson, R. 1965. *Silent spring*. London: Penguin.

Centre for Housing, Building and Planning of the Department of Economic and Social Affairs of the United Nations 1976. *Global review of human settlements*. Oxford: Pergamon.

Centro Internacional de Formación en Ciencias Ambientales (CIFCA) 1978. *Una experiencia de ecodesarrollo, el caso de Santa Marta, Colombia*. Madrid: Cuadernos del CIFCA.

Chan, G. L. 1972. *Conditioning of wastes for aquaculture*. Wellington: FAO, Indo-Pacific Fisheries Council.

Chan, G. L. 1973. *Integrated rural development (water–waste–fuel–food cycle): eight-point development plan*. Papua New Guinea: Department of Agriculture.

Cheremisinoff, P. N. and A. C. Morresi 1977. *Environmental assessment and impact statement handbook*. Ann Arbor: Ann Arbor Science.

Clapham, W. B., Jr. 1981. *Human ecosystems*. New York: Macmillan.

Clark, B. D., R. Bisset and P. Wathern 1980. *Environmental impact assessment – a bibliography with abstracts*. London: Mansell.

Cole, H. S. D., C. Freeman, M. Jahoda and K. L. R. Pavitt (eds.) 1973. *Models of doom*. New York: Universe Books.

Colinvaux, P. 1973. *Introduction to ecology*. New York: Wiley.

Collier, B. D., G. W. Cox, A. W. Johnson and P. C. Miller 1973. *Dynamic ecology*. London: Prentice-Hall.

Commonwealth Science Council 1977. *Seminar on alternative energy resources and their potential in rural development*. London.

Conant, T. *et al.* (eds.) 1983. *Resource inventories and baseline study methods for developing countries*. Washington, D.C.: American Association for the Advancement of Science.

Cooper, C. 1981. *Economic evaluation and the environment*. London: Hodder and Stoughton.

Cooper, J. B. (ed.) 1975. *Photosynthesis and productivity in different environments*. Cambridge: Cambridge University Press.

Cornell University 1974. *Processing and management of agriculture waste*. Proceedings of Cornell Agricultural Waste Management Conference, Rochester.

Council on Environmental Quality and Department of State 1980. *The global 2000 report to the President: entering the twenty-first century*, vol. 1. Washington, D.C.

Curry-Lindahl, K. 1972. *Conservation for survival: an ecological strategy*. New York: William Morrow.

Das Gupta, A. K. and D. W. Pearce 1972. *Cost–benefit analysis: theory and practice*. London: Macmillan.

Dasmann, R. F. 1963. *The last horizon*. New York: Collier Books.

Delucchi, V. L. (ed.) 1976. *Studies in biological control*. Cambridge: Cambridge University Press.

Eckholm, E. P. 1977. *The picture of health: environmental sources of disease*. New York: Norton.

Ehrlich, P. R., A. H. Ehrlich and J. P. Holdren 1973. *Human ecology*. San Francisco: W. H. Freeman.

Ehrlich, P. R., A. H. Ehrlich and J. P. Holdren 1977. *Ecoscience: population, resources, environment*. San Francisco: W. H. Freeman.

El-Hinnawi, E. 1981. *The environmental impacts of production and use of energy: an assessment prepared by the United Nations Environment Programme*. Dublin: Tycooly.

El-Hinnawi, E. and M. H. Hashmi (eds.) 1982. *Global environmental issues, United Nations Environment Programme*. Dublin: Tycooly.

Environmental Coordinating Unit (UN ESCAP) 1980. Role of environmental legislations and institutions in environmental management in the ESCAP region. In *Readings in environmental management*. Bangkok: United Nations Asian and Pacific Development Institute.

Environmental Development Action in the Third World (ENDA, Dakar) 1981. *Environment and development in Africa*. Oxford: Pergamon.

Epstein, E. *et al*. 1980. Saline culture of crops: a genetic approach. *Science* **210**, 399–404.

Food and Agriculture Organization of the United Nations (FAO) 1978. *China: recycling of organic wastes in agriculture*. FAO Soils Bull., no. 40.

Food and Agriculture Organization of the United Nations (FAO) and United Nations Environment Programme (UNEP) 1975. *The development and application of integrated pest control in agriculture*. Rome: FAO.

Frenkiel, F. N. and D. W. Goodall (eds.) 1978. *Simulation modelling of environmental problems*. SCOPE Report 9. Chichester: Wiley.

Furlan, G., N. A. Mancini and A. A. M. Sayigh (eds.) 1984. *Nonconventional energy*. New York: Plenum Press.

Golden, J., R. P. Ouelette, S. Saari and P. N. Cheremisinoff 1979. *Environmental impact data book*. Ann Arbor: Ann Arbor Science.

Goldsmith, *et al*. 1972. *Blueprint for survival*. Boston: Houghton Mifflin.

Gruhl, H. 1975. *Ein Planet wird geplündert. Die Schreckensbilanz unserer Politik*. Frankfurt: Fischer.

Harris, D. R. 1971. The ecology of swidden cultivation in the upper Orinoco rainforest, Venezuela. *Geog. Rev*. **61**, 475–95.

Holdgate, M. W., M. Kassas and G. F. White (eds.) 1982. *The world environment 1972–1982: a report by the United Nations Environment Programme*. Dublin: Tycooly.

Huffaker, C. B. (ed.) 1971. *Biological control*. New York: Plenum Press.

ILO International Labour Office 1977. *Employment, growth and basic needs: a one-world problem*. New York: Praeger.

Imboden, N. 1978. *A management approach to project appraisal and evaluation*. Paris: OECD.

International Union for Conservation of Nature and Natural Resources (IUCN) 1980. *World conservation strategy*.

Isard, W. *et al*. 1972. *Ecologic–economic analysis for regional development*. New York: The Free Press.

Islam, N. and G. M. Henault 1979. From GNP to basic needs: a critical review of development and development administration. *Int. Rev. Admin. Sci.* **XLV**(3), 253–67.

Jolly, R. 1977. Changing views on development. In *Surveys for development: a multidisciplinary approach*, J. J. Nossin (ed.), 19–35. Amsterdam: Elsevier.

Jorgensen, S. E. (ed.) 1979. *State-of-the-art in ecological modelling*. Oxford: Pergamon.

Khan, A. Z. M. O. 1980. Participatory development: the need for structural reform and people's organisation. In United Nations Asian and Pacific Development Institute (1980), 57–84.

Korten, D. C. 1980. Community organization and rural development: a learning process approach. *Publ. Admin. Rev.* **5**, 480–511.

Kothari, R. 1980. Environment and alternative development. *Alternatives* **V**(4), 427–75.

Lanly, J.-P. 1982. *Les ressources forestières tropicales*, Etude FAO: Forêts. Rome: FAO.

Lee-Smith, D. 1978. *Ecosystem approach to human settlements planning*. Revised draft (mimeographed).

Leontief, W. 1970. *Environmental repercussions and the economic structure: an input–output approach*. Rev. Econ. Stat., no. 52.

Leopold, L. B. *et al*. 1971. A procedure for evaluating environmental impact. *Geo. Surv. Circ.* **645**.

Levy, E. M. 1984. Oil pollution in the world's oceans. *Ambio* **XIII**(4), 226–35.

Lloyd, P. 1979. *Slums of hope? Shanty towns of the Third World*. Manchester: Manchester University Press.

Lo, F.-C. and K. Salih 1981. Growth poles, agropolitan development, and polarization reversal: the debate and search for alternatives. In Stöhr and Taylor (1981), 123–52.

Loraine, J. A. C. 1972. *The death of tomorrow*. London: Heinemann.

Love, G. A. and R. M. Love (eds.) 1970. *Ecological crisis: readings for survival*. New York: Harcourt Brace Jovanovich.

Lowry, K. and R. A. Carpenter 1984. *Holistic nature and fragmented bureaucracies: a study of government organization for natural systems management*. Honolulu: East–West Center.

McGarry, M. G. and J. Stainforth (eds.) 1978. *Compost, fertilizer, and biogas production from human and farm wastes in the People's Republic of China*. Ottawa: International Development Research Centre.

McHale, J. and M. C. McHale 1977. *Basic human needs: a framework for action*. New Brunswick: Transaction Books.

McNaughton, W. and L. L. Wolf 1973. *General ecology*. New York: Holt, Rinehart and Winston.

Marcelle, R. (ed.) 1975. *Environmental biological control of photosynthesis*. The Hague: W. Junk.

Meadows, D. H., D. L. Meadows, J. Randers and W. W. Behrens III 1972. *The limits to growth*. New York: Universe Books.

Montgomery, E., J. W. Bennett and T. Scudder 1977. The impact of human activities on the physical and social environment: new directions in anthropological ecology. In *Ecosocial systems and ecopolitics: a reader on human and social implications of environmental management in developing countries*, K. W. Deutsch (ed.), 77–114. Paris: UNESCO.

Morales, H. L. 1978. *La revolución azul? Aquacultura y ecodesarrollo*. Mexico: Editorial Nueva Imagen.

Morgan, R. P. and L. J. Icerman 1981. *Renewable resource utilization for development*. New York: Pergamon Press.

Mueller-Dombois, D., K. Kartawinata and L. L. Handley 1983. Conservation of species and habitat: a major responsibility in development planning. In *Natural systems for development: what planners need to know*, R. A. Carpenter (ed.), 1–51. New York: Macmillan.

Munn, R. E. (ed.) 1975. *Environmental impact assessment: principles and procedures*. SCOPE Report 5, Toronto.

Munn, R. E. (ed.) 1979. *Environmental impact assessment: principles and procedures*. Chichester: Wiley.

National Academy of Sciences 1976. *Energy for rural development: renewable resources and alternative technologies for developing countries*. Washington, D.C.

Neal, R. A. 1984. Aquaculture expansion and environmental considerations. *Mazingira* **VIII** (3), 24–8.

Nerfin, M. (ed.) 1977. *Another development: approaches and strategies*. Uppsala: Dag Hammarskjöld Foundation.

Nordhaus, W. D. and J. Tobin 1973. Is growth obsolete? *Studies in Income and Wealth* **38**, 509–64.

Odum, E. P. 1971. *Fundamentals of ecology*, 3rd edn. Philadelphia: W. B. Saunders.

Omer, S. 1980. Participatory democracy, institution building and social development. In United Nations Asian and Pacific Development Institute (1980), 113–31.

Organisation for Economic Co-operation and Development (OECD) 1973. *List of social concerns common to most OECD countries*. Paris: OECD.

Organisation for Economic Co-operation and Development (OECD) 1975. *The polluter-pays principle*. Paris: OECD.

Organisation for Economic Co-operation and Development (OECD) 1982. *Economic and ecological interdependence*. Paris: OECD.

Organisation for Economic Co-operation and Development (OECD) 1985. *The state of the environment in OECD member countries*. Paris: OECD.

Organization of American States (OAS) 1984. *Integrated regional development planning: guidelines and case studies from OAS experience*. Washington, D.C.

Organization of American States (OAS), Secretary General 1978. *Environmental quality and river basin development: a model for integrated analysis and planning*. Washington, D.C.

Ott, W. R. (ed.) 1976. *Environmental modeling and simulation*. Proceedings of the Conference on Environmental Modeling and Simulation, Cincinnati, 19–22 April 1976. Washington, D.C.: U.S. Environmental Protection Agency.

Pantulu, V. B. 1982. A case-study of the Pa Mong Project: environmental aspects. In UNEP (1982), 145–59.

Pearce, D. W. 1976. *Environmental economics*. London: Longman.

Porteous, A. 1977. *Recycling resources refuse*. London: Longman.

Pringle, L. 1971. *Ecology: science of survival*. New York: Macmillan.

Reddy, A. K. N. 1979. *Technology, development and the environment: a reappraisal*. Nairobi: UNEP.

República de Colombia, Instituto Nacional de los Recursos Naturales Renovables y del Ambiente 1980. *Programa de ecodesarrollo de Santa Marta-Colombia – formulación preliminar del programa*. Bogotá.

Riddell, R. 1981. *Ecodevelopment, economics, ecology and development: an alternative to growth-imperative models*. Westmead: Gower.

Romanini, C. 1974. *Quelques écotechniques pour le tropique humide*. Cahiers de l'Ecodéveloppement, no. 1. Paris: Centre International de Recherche sur l'Environnement et le Développement.

Royal Society of Canada 1974. *Waste recycling and the environment*. Ottawa.

Ruddle, K. and W. Manshard 1981. *Renewable natural resources and the environment: pressing problems in the developing world*. Dublin: Tycooly.

Russel, C. S., W. O. Spofford and E. T. Haefele 1974. The management of the quality of the environment. In *The management of water quality and the environment*, J. Rothenberg and J. G. Heggie (eds.). New York: Halsted Press.

Sachs, I. 1976. Environment and styles of development. In *Outer limits and human needs*, W. H. Matthews (ed.), 41–65. Uppsala: Dag Hammarskjöld Foundation.

Sachs, I. 1980. *Stratégies de l'écodéveloppement*. Paris: Editions ouvrières.

Sachs, I. 1982. Environment and development revisited: ten years after the Stockholm Conference. *Alternatives* **8**, 369–78.

Sametz, A. W. 1968. Production of goods and services, the measurement of economic growth. In *Indicators of social change: concepts and measurements*, E. B. Sheldon and W. E. Moore (eds.), 77–95. New York: Russell Sage Foundation.

Sargent II, F. 1974. *Human ecology*. Amsterdam: North-Holland.

Schneier, G. and K. Vinaver 1979. *Ecodéveloppement et habitat: quelques éléments de reflexion*. Paris: Centre International de Recherche sur l'Environnement et le Développement.

Schumacher, E. F. 1973. *Small is beautiful: economics as if people mattered*. New York: Harper and Row.

Seers, D. (ed.) 1981. *Dependency theory: a critical reassessment*. London: Frances Pinter.

Seers, D. 1983. *The political economy of nationalism*. London: Oxford University Press.

Shubert, C. 1982. Environmental improvement of marginal urban settlements in Indonesia and the Philippines. In UNEP (1982), 259–75.

Sigal, S. 1979. *Elements for a new health strategy in Third World countries*. Ecodevelopment Study, no. 10. Paris: Centre International de Recherche sur l'Environnement et le développement.

Simon, J. L. and H. Kahn (eds.) 1984. *The resourceful Earth: a response to Global 2000*. Oxford: Blackwell.

Smith, R. L. 1972. *The ecology of man: an ecosystem approach*. New York: Harper and Row.

Soedjatmoko 1979. National policy implications of the basic-needs model. *Development Digest* **XVII**(3), 55–68.

Sorensen, B. 1979. *Renewable energy*. London: Academic Press.

Spofford, W. O. 1973. Total environmental quality management models. In *Models for environmental pollution control*, R. A. Deininger (ed.), 403–43. Ann Arbor: Ann Arbor Science.

Statistical Office of the Department of Economic and Social Affairs of the United Nations 1976. *Global review of human settlements, statistical annex*. Oxford: Pergamon Press.

Statistisk Sentralbyrå 1981. *Ressursregnskap, resource accounts*. Oslo.

Stöhr, W. B. 1981. Development from below: the bottom-up and periphery-inward development paradigm. In Stöhr and Taylor (1981), 39–72.

Stöhr, W. B. and D. R. F. Taylor (eds.) 1981. *Development from above or below: the dialectics of regional planning in developing countries.* New York: Wiley.

Stokes, B. 1978. *Local responses to global problems: a key to meeting basic human needs.* Worldwatch Paper, no. 17.

Suriyakumaran, C. (ed.) 1980. *Environmental assessment statements: a test model presentation.* Bangkok: UNEP, Regional Office for Asia and the Pacific and United Nations Asian and Pacific Development Institute.

Todaro, M. P. 1977. *Economic development in the Third World: an introduction to problems and policies in a global perspective.* London: Longman.

Turk, A., J. Turk, J. T. Wittes and R. Wittes 1974. *Environmental science.* Philadelphia: W. B. Saunders.

Umweltbundesamt (ed.) 1978. *UMPLIS, Verzeichnis rechengestützter Umweltmodelle.* Berlin: Erich Schmidt.

United Nations 1973. *Report of the United Nations Conference on the Human Environment.* New York: United Nations.

United Nations 1976. *Report of Habitat: United Nations Conference on Human Settlements.* New York: United Nations.

United Nations 1978a. *Social indicators: preliminary guidelines and illustrative series.* Statistical Papers, Ser. M No. 63. New York: United Nations.

United Nations 1978b. *Water development and management: proceedings of the United Nations Water Conference Mar del Plata, Argentina, March 1977.* Oxford: Pergamon.

United Nations 1981. *World statistics in brief.* New York: United Nations.

United Nations 1982a. *Survey of environment statistics: frameworks, approaches and statistical publications.* New York: United Nations.

United Nations 1982b. *Towards the new international economic order: report of the Director General for Development and International Economic Cooperation.* New York: United Nations.

United Nations 1983a. *Directory of environment statistics.* New York: United Nations.

United Nations 1983b. *The law of the sea.* New York: United Nations.

United Nations 1984. *Crisis or reform: breaking the barriers to development.* New York: United Nations.

United Nations Asian and Pacific Development Institute 1980. *Local level planning and rural development: alternative strategies.* New Delhi: Concept Publishing.

United Nations Conference on the Human Environment, Report and Working Papers of a Panel of Experts 1972. *Development and environment.* Mouton: United Nations and Ecole Pratique des Hautes Etudes.

United Nations Conference on Trade and Development (UNCTAD) 1984. *The least developed countries, 1984 report.* New York: United Nations.

United Nations, Economic and Social Commission for Asia and the

Pacific (UN ESCAP) 1985. *State of the environment in Asia and the Pacific*. Bangkok.

United Nations Economic Commission for Europe (UN ECE) 1978. *Non-waste technology and production*. Oxford: Pergamon.

United Nations Educational, Scientific and Cultural Organization (UNESCO) 1981a. *Programme on man and the biosphere (MAB): international workshop on ecological problems of human settlements in arid lands*. MAB report series, no. 54.

United Nations Educational, Scientific and Cultural Organization (UNESCO) 1981b. *International Co-ordinating Council of the programme on man and the biosphere (MAB)*. MAB report series, no. 53.

United Nations Environment Programme (UNEP) 1975. *The proposed programme*. (UNEP/GC/3) Nairobi.

United Nations Environment Programme (UNEP) 1976. *Ecodevelopment*. (UNEP/GC/80) Nairobi.

United Nations Environment Programme (UNEP) 1978. *Review of the areas environment and development and environmental management*. Nairobi: UNEP.

United Nations Environment Programme (UNEP) 1979. *Directory of institutions and individuals active in environmentally-sound and appropriate technologies*. Oxford: Pergamon Press.

United Nations Environment Programme (UNEP) 1982. *Environment and development in Asia and the Pacific: experience and prospects*. Nairobi: UNEP.

United Nations Environment Programme (UNEP) 1984. *Annual report of the Executive Director 1983*. Nairobi: UNEP.

United Nations Environment Programme (UNEP), Food and Agriculture Organization of the United Nations (FAO) 1977. *Residue utilization management of agricultural and agro-industrial residues*. Rome.

United Nations Environment Programme (UNEP) and United Nations Conference on Trade and Development (UNCTAD), Symposium on "Patterns of resource use, environment and development strategy" 1974. *The Cocoyoc Declaration* (mimeographed). Cocoyoc.

United Nations Industrial Development Organization (UNIDO) 1979. *Conceptual and policy framework for appropriate industrial technology*. New York: United Nations.

United Nations World Food Council 1977. *Eradicating hunger and malnutrition*. Report by the Executive Director, Third Session, Manila.

U.S. Department of Commerce, National Technical Information Service (NTIS) 1983. *Bibliography of appropriate technology information for developing countries*, 4th edn. Springfield: NTIS.

U.S. Environmental Protection Agency 1977. *Summaries of foreign government environmental reports*. Washington, D.C.

U.S. Federal Interagency Task Force on Air Quality Indicators 1976. *A recommended air pollution index*. Washington, D.C.

Van den Bosch, R. and P. S. Messenger 1973. *Biological control*. New York: Intext Educational Publishers.

Walters, C. J. 1978. Obergurgl: development in high mountain regions of Austria. In *Adaptive environmental assessment and management*, C. S. Holling (ed.). Chichester: Wiley.

Walters, C. J. and R. M. Peterman 1978. Simulation Modeling. In *Adaptive environmental assessment and management*, C. S. Holling (ed.). Chichester: Wiley.

Weatherly, W. P. 1983. Insect Pest Outbreaks. In *Natural systems for development: what planners need to know*, R. A. Carpenter (ed.), 299–334. New York: Macmillan.

Weber, R. D. 1982. *Energy information guide, Volume I. General and alternative energy sources*. Santa Barbara: ABC-CLIO.

World Bank 1973. *Environmental, health and human ecologic considerations in economic development projects*. Washington, D.C.: World Bank.

World Bank 1982. *Tribal peoples and economic development: human ecologic considerations*. Washington, D.C.: World Bank.

World Health Organization (WHO) 1978. *Primary health care*. Report of the International Conference on Primary Health Care, Alma Ata, 6–12 September 1978, Geneva.

Index

Numbers printed in bold type indicate where terms are just introduced, or defined.